ADVANCE PRAISE

"A must-read for the modern marketer or PE operating partner. As the buyer journey has been fundamentally reshaped, legacy tactics are no longer effective, and a new playbook has emerged. Winning today requires driving awareness and becoming a trusted source of insight—often without the web traffic we once took for granted. As attention shifts toward AI-driven discovery, earning external share of voice is essential. Shiv masterfully lays out how to do exactly that."

—RYAN BRADY, PRINCIPAL, HEAD OF VALUE
CREATION AT UPDATA PARTNERS

"Marketing and demand generation are changing fast. Funnel dynamics are shifting, and staying ahead requires a fundamentally new approach. Shiv does an outstanding job simplifying and demystifying the changes every business is facing today. His seven-step blueprint is an actionable guide for marketers who don't just want to keep up but want to win in the new world of the AI-driven buyer's journey."

—RAY WIZBOWSKI, CMO OF ECI SOFTWARE SOLUTIONS

"Shiv has a rare ability to strip marketing down to what actually matters. AI Marketing Blueprint cuts away the noise, clarifies what's changed, and shows how the pieces fit together. Shiv offers marketing leaders a systems-based framework for structuring strategy, investment, and execution so marketing functions as a cohesive whole—not a collection of disconnected tactics."

—JON PENLAND, CEO OF KINSTA

"Shiv has a wealth of knowledge in helping companies focus their revenue efforts across content, channels, and tech. Marketing has changed substantially with AI adoption and the rapid decline in results from traditional tactics. AI Marketing Blueprint is an essential guide for every marketer: it's a concrete approach to transitioning to the new marketing model that returns you to growth."

—HOLLY SIMMONS, CMO OF OUTREACH

"I've seen first-hand how Shiv's marketing frameworks transform revenue generation. As growth becomes more complex in an AI-driven world, AI Marketing Blueprint offers an actionable solution and is essential reading for any investor, CEO or marketing leader."'

—BRYCE YOUNGREN, MANAGING PARTNER
AT POLARIS GROWTH FUND

"In a world where AI is rewriting the rules of engagement faster than most teams can update their playbooks, AI Marketing Blueprint delivers exactly what modern marketers need: clarity, structure, and practical guidance."

—STACY WEST, CMO OF BONTERRA

"Working with Shiv, I've come to rely on his straightforward style of taking complex marketing problems and turning them into clear frameworks that drive real results. This book replaces vague 'AI marketing' advice with concrete, measurable approaches to keep up with changing buyer behavior and channel shifts while driving pipeline and revenue."

—LACEY FORD, CMO OF ABC FITNESS

"I've spent my career evaluating what drives durable growth and value creation in private companies. Shiv cuts through the hype around AI and translates it into a clear and implementable framework for building real pipeline and revenue. If you care about results, this is required reading."

—ZANE TARENCE, PARTNER AND MANAGING DIRECTOR AT FOUNDERS ADVISORS

"In a market that keeps changing, leaders need to learn how to evolve. AI Marketing Blueprint is a core resource for understanding the impact of AI and refocusing your business. Shiv helps you build the foundation for success with a strategic approach to transforming marketing and driving revenue."

—DAN CREMONS, FOUNDER OF ACCELERA PARTNERS

"AI has made much more of the buyer journey invisible. We can't observe intent the way we used to, and the observable trail marketers historically relied on is disappearing. That makes brand essential: perception is reality. The companies that win with AI deliberately choose what they want to be known for and make that visible through citable content, narrative, and trust. AI Marketing Blueprint is a hands-on guide for teams that want a real roadmap—not just theory—on how to operate in this new reality."

—CAROLINE TARPEY, MANAGING DIRECTOR AT LEAD EDGE CAPITAL

"Shiv's done it again—another deeply strategic and relentlessly practical guide for modern Go-To-Market teams. AI Marketing Blueprint is a comprehensive, hands-on manual for the new reality of B2B growth. It's not theoretical—it's operational.

"Buyer behavior has changed faster than most Go-To-Market models. Shiv cuts through the noise and lays out an actionable framework built for how people buy in an AI-first world. Every chapter is grounded in real behavior and focused on what matters: protecting pipeline, rebuilding demand, and creating a durable advantage.

"You may have been successful with the old way of marketing. AI Marketing Blueprint explains why that's no longer enough—and how to build what comes next.

"This isn't a book you read once. It's a playbook you run again and again."

—JENNIFER MONTAGUE, FORMER SENIOR DIRECTOR
OF GTM AT VERDANE AND AI ADOPTION LEADER

AI MARKETING BLUEPRINT

7 NEW RULES FOR DRIVING PIPELINE AND REVENUE

Shiv Narayanan

AI MARKETING BLUEPRINT
7 New Rules for Driving Pipeline and Revenue

FIRST EDITION

ISBN   978-1-5445-5200-2   *Hardcover*
       978-1-5445-5199-9   *Paperback*
       978-1-5445-5201-9   *Ebook*

CONTENTS

DISCLAIMER

All the stories in this book are real, from situations we encounter every day with our clients at How To SaaS. Details—companies, people, products, revenue numbers, market intelligence, financials—have been altered and fictionalized to preserve confidentiality and protect sensitive information. All examples, metrics, and data are used for illustrative purposes only.

INTRODUCTION

THE GREAT MARKETING DISRUPTION

"Our lead volume has declined by 28 percent in the last few quarters. Traffic, leads, and MQLs are all down. We need to figure out what's going wrong," said Peter, the CEO of ServiceFlow, cutting straight to the point.

Sarah, ServiceFlow's Chief Marketing Officer, was also on the call with her quarterly report pulled up on her screen, showing the troubling trends across their $25 million field service management platform.

"Help me understand the full picture," I replied, settling into my chair. "Walk me through the specific numbers you're seeing."

Sarah took the lead on the data. "Our organic traffic has dropped 35 percent over the past 12 months—from 147,000 monthly visitors in Q1 2024 down to 96,000 in Q4. But here's what's puzzling:

our content is still ranking well, our technical SEO is solid, and our domain authority hasn't changed."

"What about paid media performance?" I asked.

"That's even more concerning," Sarah continued. "Our cost per click is up 47 percent year-over-year, click-through rates are down 23 percent, and our customer acquisition cost has increased by 62 percent. We initially blamed iOS updates and privacy changes, but those effects stabilized months ago."

Peter jumped in, his frustration evident. "The part that doesn't make sense is that the prospects who do reach us are more qualified than we've ever seen. Our sales team consistently reports that leads are coming in more educated about their needs. But there are just fewer of them."

"What about Generative Search and AI platforms?" I asked.

"We've been working with our agency on that," Sarah explained. "They've been encouraging us to keep working on SEO fundamentals so that AI platforms also rank us well."

"Is that working?" I pushed.

Sarah paused and then finally said, "I'm not sure."

"Last question," I said. "How much of your traffic, leads, and pipeline has historically come from inbound?"

"About 60–70 percent," replied Sarah.

"Do me a favor—let's pull up some visibility metrics," I said. I had a pretty strong idea of what the problem was. "I want to know to figure out how often you're showing up on these AI platforms."

I worked with Sarah to get the underlying numbers. What we found was alarming. ServiceFlow was showing up less than 10 percent of the time in AI answers for the queries it would want to rank for on AI Overviews and Generative Search results. At the same time, Branded Search volumes had declined by almost 30 percent.

This was all I needed to see. It was the same problem I'd been seeing across several of our clients at How To SaaS. For years, they had built a thriving $25 million business that relied on Google Search, SEO, and ads to drive growth.

Their mistake? They almost took it for granted as a channel they would invest in and find more leads each month. When AI platforms took over in 2024, everything shifted.

"We're going to need to shift how you think about Marketing at ServiceFlow," I said to Peter and Sarah.

"What do you mean?" asked Peter.

"I feel like we've been doing a pretty good job," said Sarah, defensively.

"You've been doing a good job with the old way of doing things," I replied. "You need to build a Marketing model for the new way of doing things now."

CHANGING CUSTOMER BEHAVIOR

What Sarah and Peter had missed was a critical shift in how customers were making purchasing decisions.

"Let me ask you something. How often are you using Google today compared to 3 years ago?"

Peter thought for a moment. "I use it a lot still, but not nearly as much as I used to," he admitted. "I often find myself using ChatGPT or Gemini when I want to look up something quickly."

"Exactly," I said. "You're doing exactly the same thing your customers are doing."

Peter had said the quiet part out loud. Users were searching for more and more things on AI platforms, but Google still held a majority share of the market. As of Q2 2025, nearly 6 percent of US search traffic was going to AI platforms, according to Datos (and this number is climbing rapidly). Gartner predicts this volume will increase to 25 percent or more in 2026. Meanwhile, ChatGPT, Gemini, Claude, and other AI platforms have seen user growth explode every year since their launch.

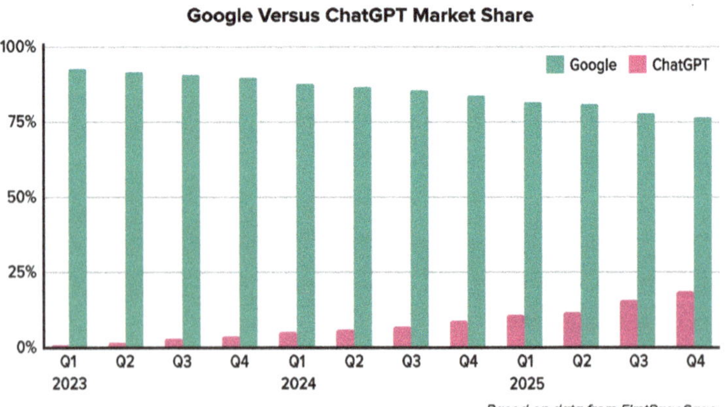

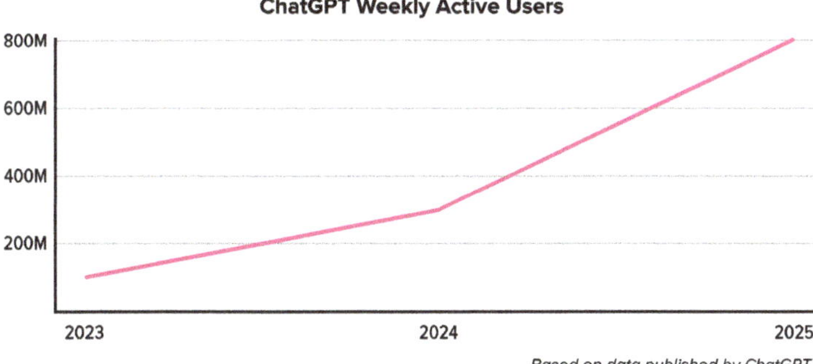

Zero-Click Searches have also been on the rise. This means that even when customers search on Google, they bounce before clicking links to companies trying to address those needs or sell a product.

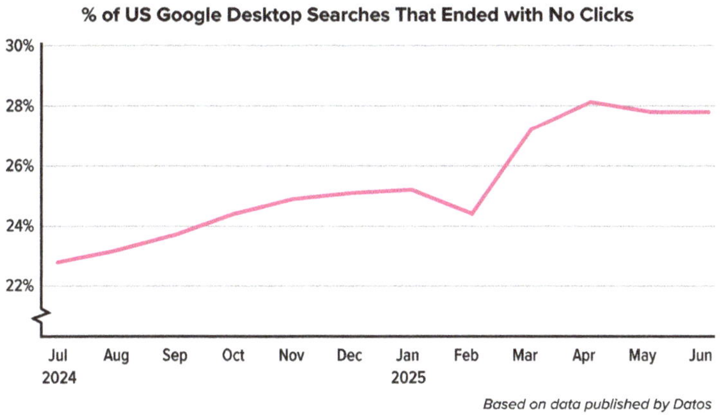

ServiceFlow wasn't alone in this trend, impacting its business. The reality of this shift meant declining growth and margins for all kinds of companies. HubSpot and Monday both reported significant declines in inbound volumes and saw their stock prices plummet as a result.

"This represents a major existential threat for your business," I explained to Peter and Sarah. "You've historically had 60–70 percent of your growth driven by search. And now that channel is rapidly declining."

Peter looked worried, "Are you saying it's going to get worse?"

"Yes, it will certainly get worse, but only if we don't fix it," I replied. "The urgency is high because there is a legitimate threat to business continuity."

"How do we fix it?" asked Sarah. I could sense the urgency in her voice.

"By meeting customers where they are."

UNDERSTANDING THE NEW BUYER JOURNEY

In the last 15 years, B2B buyer journeys have shifted significantly.

In a pre-inbound world, sales reps were how buyers educated themselves through to a purchasing decision. They would meet BDRs or SDRs, who would qualify them and then introduce them to Account Executives. The AEs would run the process from demo to close. Marketing would support with traditional methods such as events, sales enablement, PR, and corporate marketing.

When Google Search rose to prominence, customers began slowly researching more and more. This led to the birth of inbound marketing, as popularized by HubSpot. Problem recognition led to Google searches, which led to website visits, content downloads, email nurturing sequences, and eventually sales conversations. The entire process was still quite linear and trackable.

Then came the rise of social media. Customers were not only researching on Google; they also began consuming content at alarming rates. Connecting with audiences on social became essential to layer on top of inbound, as a way to distinguish yourself in a crowded marketplace.

Customers stopped following a linear buyer. Instead, they skip back and forth between stages and interact with businesses on different platforms.

Suddenly, attribution became a hot-button topic. What gets the credit when customers jump back and forth across so many channels, programs, and touchpoints? What should you scale up or down? Companies began obsessing over multi-touch attribution to answer this question. From 2021 to 2023, it was the best time to be a marketing attribution software company because everyone believed better tracking was the answer to their marketing problems.

Turns out, they were all wrong. The customer does not care what your attribution model says about which channels have the biggest impact. The customer cares about making the best possible decision, and they will go to the path of least resistance to get as much information as possible to make the right decision for their circumstances. They will search on Google, read Reddit threads and Capterra reviews, attend your (and your competitors') webinar, watch a YouTube video by someone comparing your solution to other options, read case studies, talk to references, and much more to figure out if you are the right solution for their situation.

It is a lot of work for buyers to take on. They took on the sales reps' responsibilities in 2010 by doing the work themselves. They'll do it for small decisions like which $200 headphones to buy, and they'll do it for large decisions like which $25,000 software to buy.

Which brings us to where we are now—AI and LLM platforms are helping customers educate themselves even more. What once required a complicated Google Search, checking multiple websites, doing your own research, and making a decision can now be done in seconds.

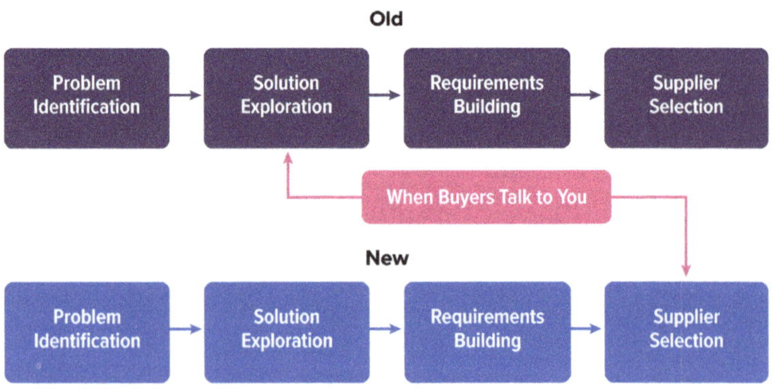

And they trust the AI platforms—this is the key point. They trust the AI platforms like they would their best friend, consigliere, fiduciary, and trustee.

The customer doesn't need to put in the same amount of effort or time to do their research. AI platforms do the laborious work for them. They no longer have to second-guess if a sales rep truly has their best interests at heart in a conversation because the AI platform is that and more for them.

All of this is a trend towards the democratization of knowledge, education, and resources that empowers people to make better decisions in every area of their lives. Want to figure out the best Indian restaurant in your city? Don't check Yelp, just ask ChatGPT. Want to know which golf clubs you should buy based on your yardages and handicap? Don't read Reddit threads, just ask ChatGPT. Want to figure out which CRM is the best for your business? Don't search on Google, just ask ChatGPT.

"This is the new reality for all companies," I explained to Peter and Sarah. "You have to build companies for a world where buyers and customers are constantly educating themselves without talking to you."

THE LONG-TAIL OF SELF-EDUCATION

"What follows is going to be more of the same, on steroids," I continued. "You're not going to see less of it; you will see more of it."

I could see the wheels turning for Peter and Sarah. They were beginning to understand what this all meant.

"Everything will move to a long-tail of self-education," I explained.

"What do you mean?" asked Sarah.

"Your customers are going to educate themselves with extremely detailed queries that were previously not possible in a world of search."

In the old world of Search, long-tail meant seven- to fifteen-word queries. For example, "Top 10 field service management software solutions for roofing companies." ServiceFlow had done well to rank for terms like this on Google.

In a world with AI, everything moves to the extreme long tail. This means customers are doing deep research at every stage of the buyer journey, without interacting with you or your business in any way. All the education is happening on the platform itself.

- Instead of coming to your homepage, they ask AI what your solution does and if it's a good fit for them
- Instead of coming to your pricing page, they ask AI to evaluate all the tools in your space, along with pricing, ROI calculations, and making a business case
- Instead of reading reviews on sites like Capterra and G2, they ask AI to summarize your and your competitors' reviews in a summary table
- Instead of scheduling a demo with you and competitors, they ask AI to build a full feature comparison table with pros and cons

Think about all the work you are doing to create product marketing, sales enablement, and education content for your website and your sales team that is likely to never be seen by the customer in this world.

The result is declining performance across the board because your business never sees any of these interactions. Numbers across all analytics and attribution tools plummet at every stage of the customer journey. This is what is actually happening:

Stage of Journey	Old Behavior	New Behavior	Outcome
Problem Identification	Searches short queries on Google	Asks ChatGPT/Gemini several questions	Decline in top of funnel SEO traffic
Solution Exploration	Goes to multiple review websites, comes to your website, clicks around	Asks AI platforms to compile a short list of options/solutions	Lower traffic from Capterra, G2, or your solution pages
Requirements Building	Looks through all features and benefits, uses RFPs, advisors	Asks AI platforms to compile full lists of requirements to their specific scenario/budget	Lower MQLs/demos/show-up rates
Supplier Selection	Runs through long internal review cycles to build a business case	Asks AI to build the business case	Higher close rates for winners, plummeting close rates for everyone else

This is why, if you are optimizing only for Search, your business will die. And it will happen whether you like it or not.

"Help me understand this," said Peter. "You want us to build in a way that doesn't encourage customers to come to our website?"

"Sounds crazy, right?" I said affirmatively.

"Yes, it sounds insane," said Sarah, chiming in.

"Here's the difference," I expanded. "If you do it this way, you'll get more website traffic than ever before."

Peter and Sarah looked confused. "How?" they asked together.

"Because in a world with AI," I answered, "Branded and Direct Traffic is by far the most important traffic source."

THE VALUE OF BRANDED AND DIRECT TRAFFIC

One of the dirty secrets of a lot of Marketing departments of companies—and the agencies they work with, for that matter—is that they actually don't drive any "net new" pipeline and Demand Generation. Instead, they farm the demand that already exists. What this looks like, when you look at the metrics, is Branded terms like "ServiceFlow software" or "ServiceFlow reviews" or "ServiceFlow pricing" driving most of the traffic, demos, and revenue.

If you look at the traffic sources and attribution analytics of companies, you'll find data that looks something like this:

PAID MEDIA PERFORMANCE

CAMPAIGN	SPEND	PIPELINE FROM PAID MEDIA
Branded	25%	60%
Competitors	10%	10%
Bottom of Funnel	40%	15%
Middle of Funnel	20%	10%
Top of Funnel	5%	5%

SOURCES	TRAFFIC %
Branded Search	30%
Direct/Referral	25%
Organic Search	20%
Paid Media	15%
Organic Social	10%

When we pulled up ServiceFlow's numbers, they were freakishly close to the numbers above.

"How did you know what the splits would look like?" asked Sarah.

"Because this is what the splits look like for most companies," I responded. "I've seen the same report for thousands of companies at this point."

What's amazing about this data is that Branded Search + Direct/Referral accounted for 55 percent of the traffic at ServiceFlow, and Branded alone accounted for 60 percent of the pipeline from paid media spend.

Historically, this would be seen as a bad thing. While customers finding you through your Brand and Direct is great, it signals that the Marketing team isn't very effective. Why does a company need a Marketing team if most of the pipeline drive comes from its brand and referrals from existing customers, right?

When social media emerged as a channel, this flipped to being an incredibly good thing. Why? Because someone could see a CEO's post on LinkedIn, watch a video on YouTube, see an influencer mention your product on Instagram, and then go straight to ServiceFlow's website to buy. On attribution tools, none of those other touchpoints would be visible.

AI takes this concept and adds a whole new level of attribution complexity. At least in a world of social media, you could still track *something*. You could track video views, podcast downloads, followers, engagements from key accounts, and track website visits from people in a paid social campaign, and attribute traffic back to sources.

In an AI-first world, most of the buyer journey is invisible.

The more someone self-educates their way through AI platforms to learn about your solution, through to a purchasing decision, the less insight you will have on what they are actually doing.

"How are we ever supposed to know which of our investments made an impact?" asked Peter.

"More tools will emerge over time," I said. "The important thing to understand is that you will definitely be able to measure how you're performing based on how you see Branded, Direct, and Referral Traffic improve. If you're showing up on AI platforms as the answers to multiple queries, inevitably users will then look you up on Google or come to your website directly afterwards."

After conducting AI research, users often run a traditional Google Search or go straight to a Branded website. What's more is that the stronger your brand, the more likely AI will use you for citations. Higher brand search volume is directly correlated with AI mentions and citations, as shown in a study by Ahrefs. This is not a coincidence. Stronger brand search volumes signal to AI platforms that you can be trusted.

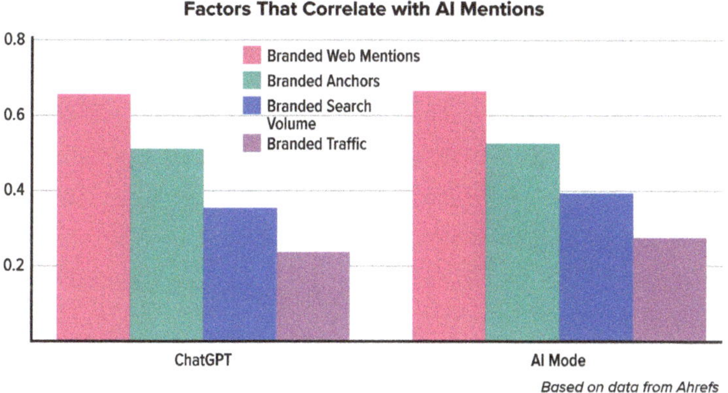

"The moment you understand this dynamic," I continued, "everything you think about Marketing and driving pipeline in an AI world will change."

"So if we optimize for the long-tail of self-education, we will see an increase in Branded Search and Direct Traffic?" asked Sarah rhetorically.

Peter was nodding as he made the same connection, "This means we've been missing out on millions of dollars in pipeline simply because we are not letting customers self-educate on these AI platforms so that they eventually come directly to us to buy."

"Bingo."

THE AI MARKETING TRANSFORMATION FRAMEWORK

Once you reach the same epiphany as Peter and Sarah, things become crystal clear. In an AI world, invisibility is the kiss of death.

The more visible you are through the long-tail of self-education, the more buyers trust your solution as it is being recommended by their most trusted advisor. The more they see you being recommended, the more they will find you directly through Branded Search and Direct website visits. The more they directly find you, the more they will buy from you without even considering competitors who are invisible.

"How do we fix this?" asked Peter.

It was a fair question. No one has really figured out what is really important in an AI world yet. Luckily, with our clients at How To SaaS, we get to see the CRM, ads, SEO, and website data of thousands of companies and have been helping them navigate through all this uncertainty. Over time, patterns emerge.

"We need to help the AI platforms realize that we have the right training data for them," I answered. "The better we do this, the more visible we'll be and the faster we'll grow."

The AI Marketing Blueprint involves understanding the seven new rules of Marketing in a world with AI:

1. **Prequalification in the Long-Tail of Self-Education:** Do everything in your power to help customers work their way through the buyer journey by themselves, without ever interacting with you, your business, your sales reps, or your website.

2. **Building Authority Through Iconic Positioning:** Invest into building authority and provide deep expertise to create a distinct brand in the marketplace.

3. **Becoming Citation Worthy as a Media Company:** Ensure your content is appearing on all platforms AI is using as training data so it can be tactically referenced for as many queries as possible.

4. **Growing a Following with Original Content:** Leverage authentic expertise to create first-party content that no one else in the market can produce and establish pre-built trust in the marketplace.

5. **Leveraging Product for Multi-Variate Problems:** Build product tools that AI platforms can leverage to create outputs inside their respective platforms for queries that cannot be solved with just content.

6. **Amplifying Reach with Paid Distribution:** Capitalize on your brand positioning and power in the marketplace to drive paid media spend and overall performance to reach your ICP efficiently.

7. **Deploying a New Sales Playbook:** Focus on intent signals created by the content engine across all platforms and co-create content with prospective buyers to drive more pipeline and revenue.

1. Prequalification	2. Iconic Positioning	3. Citation-Worthy Content	4. Authenticity and Originality
Create a list of fifteen to twenty-five long-tail self-education queries to prequalify your ICP.	*Create a list of five to ten adjacent problem areas your ICP is facing beyond the scope of your solution.*	*Identify one Anchor Content Property you will heavily invest into as a way to signal your expertise.*	*Build one proprietary process, framework, or approach to help your ICP navigate their core pain points.*

5. Product Levers	6. Paid Distribution	7. Sales Plays
Identify three to five product tools that can help your ICP solve their problems without necessarily buying your full solution.	*Choose one to two paid media channels to invest into to amplify the reach, visibility, brand recall, and affinity of your content and solution.*	*Prioritize three to five sales plays built around intent signals and cocreating content with your ICP to scale outreach, especially higher-value accounts.*

Download at howtosaas.com/blueprint

Each of these seven new rules is actually connected and intertwined with the rest. Each rule builds on the previous one to help companies increase their visibility, pipeline, and revenue in a world with AI. You need to invest in all seven areas almost simultaneously, which is why implementing the framework requires a collaborative effort across the business.

It can feel overwhelming at first. Implementing the AI Marketing Blueprint is not just another Go-To-Market initiative inside companies. It requires looking at the business in a whole new way through the lens of the customer in a world where they interact with AI platforms every single day. Getting this right requires focus and attention from the business. But if you don't invest in this, your competitors will. The businesses that evolve to meet customers where they are stand to gain significant market share. The end result of this evolution is a total business transformation—something companies need to be ready to take on.

To simplify the process, I developed the AI Marketing Blueprint as a canvas that all businesses can fill out to create a simplified view of the project's scope, the investment required, and the transformation they are about to experience.

The AI Marketing Blueprint was designed to apply to companies across all industries and verticals, regardless of their stage of maturity or revenue. The specific activities that emerge as priorities for your business will depend on your size, stage, buyer profile, and Go-To-Market. ServiceFlow completed this evolution in 12 months, but depending on the resources you have available and the opportunities this process uncovers for your business, you may be able to accelerate the timeline. The same principles apply to a company doing $500 million in revenue as to one doing $1 million in revenue. The $500 million company might be able to produce all the required content within a few months using only its in-house team, while the $1 million revenue company might use a combination of AI tools and freelancers to increase efficiency and build the right content over the course of a year.

In the chapters ahead, you'll see how I guide Peter, Sarah, and ServiceFlow through this process. In each chapter, we will work through one of the boxes in the AI Marketing Blueprint to pull together a holistic plan to capture the opportunity sitting in front of ServiceFlow and companies like yours. As we move through the ServiceFlow story, I encourage you to fill out the AI Marketing Blueprint for yourself.

You can download a fillable version of the AI Marketing Blueprint at www.howtosaas.com/blueprint. At the end of each chapter, there will be prompts to help you fill out each section so you can follow along and build an actionable roadmap for your own business.

"Let's get moving on this as soon as possible," said Peter. He understood the urgency of getting this right and the existential risk to ServiceFlow if we didn't.

Over the next 6 months, I worked with Peter and Sarah to transform how ServiceFlow approached Marketing in a world with AI. Just a year later, ServiceFlow put up record numbers for marketing performance:

- Visibility metrics on AI platforms climbed past 60 percent
- YoY Growth increased from 15 percent to 40 percent
- NRR improved from 105 percent to 115 percent
- New ARR grew by 2.5 times to $6.25 million per year
- Sales Pipeline almost doubled to $15.6 million
- Ending ARR grew to $35 million

These results aren't an anomaly. Using the AI Marketing Blueprint on our clients at How To SaaS, we've transformed thousands of other companies in different markets, verticals, and industries, and helped them create hundreds of millions of dollars in enterprise value.

It works. It will work for you too.

By the end of this book, you'll know exactly how to leverage AI to transform your Go-To-Market and start seeing Marketing as the next big value creation lever for your business.

You'll also de-risk your business continuity from the threat of AI disruption and spiraling downwards into irrelevance.

CHAPTER 1

PREQUALIFICATION IN THE LONG-TAIL OF SELF-EDUCATION

1. Prequalification

Create a list of fifteen to twenty-five long-tail self-education queries to prequalify your ICP.

Download at howtosaas.com/blueprint

"Peter, you said something earlier that caught my attention, but we never got into it," I said.

"What was that?" He asked.

"You said that your close rates are actually higher for the opportunities you are generating."

"That's right," affirmed Peter. "The deals that are coming in are closing at higher rates than before and with faster cycles."

When I looked at ServiceFlow's metrics, some amazing insights emerged:

- Close rates had jumped from 30 percent to 40 percent
- Average deal sizes had increased by 15 percent
- Sales cycles had decreased by 50 percent
- First-year retention had improved from 92 percent to 97 percent

"This has been the part that has been the most perplexing," said Peter. "Our sales efficiency has improved so much, you'd think that our top-of-funnel metrics would benefit from the same trend."

"Peter, you've inadvertently accomplished what Go-To-Market teams dream about," I said.

"What do you mean?" asked Peter.

"You've stopped targeting bad-fit customers."

This wasn't something Peter and Sarah had done consciously. AI platforms had done it for ServiceFlow instead.

In the sales-led world, BDRs and SDRs would be a buyer's first point of contact with a company. These reps would have short, thirty-minute calls with prospects to determine whether they were a good fit for a particular solution. If the prospect was a fit, the lead would be passed to an Account Executive who would manage the process through to close. The logic was simple: Don't waste expensive Account Executives on leads that will never close. Don't waste the budget on bad-fit customers.

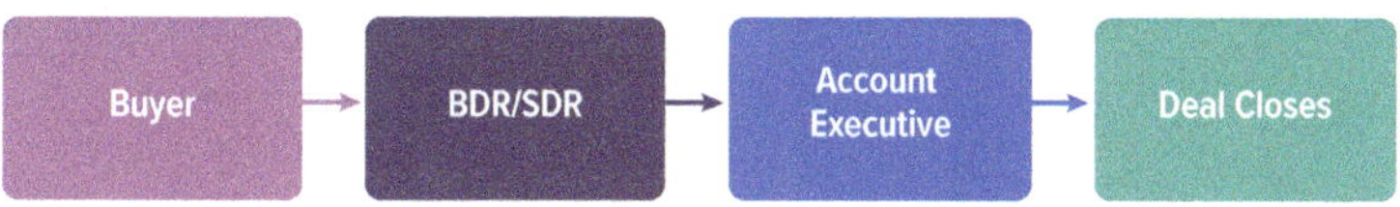

In an inbound world, this same logic continued, but a lot more noise entered the funnel. Many potential customers from adjacent verticals entered the funnel. For example, if you sold CRM to accounting firms, you would also happily take on engineering firms as clients. SDRs would still qualify, but why turn away revenue right? The features were similar enough that customers would still stay long enough to justify it.

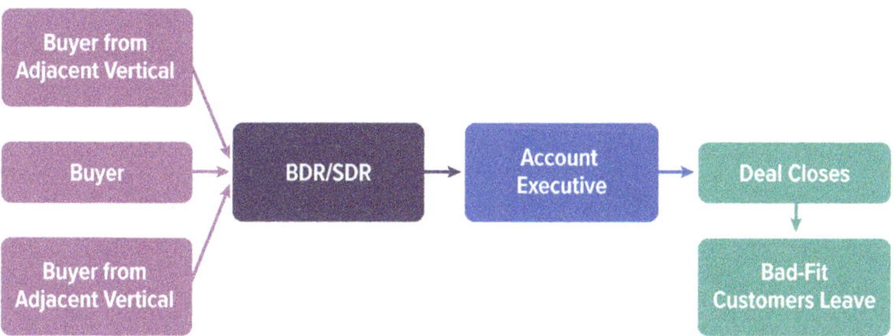

This also became a common growth strategy for most companies—to expand into adjacent verticals—and it still happens to a large extent today. The problem with this approach is that it led to a lot of waste. Most companies we come into are deploying too much of their Go-To-Market budget on customers who aren't a good fit for what they're selling. In many companies, the budget is allocated equally between bad-fit and best-fit customers, even though the revenue contribution from each segment is significantly different.

	Best-Fit	Medium-Fit	Bad-Fit
% of Customers	50%	30%	20%
% of Revenue	70%	20%	10%
% of Marketing Budget	33.33%	33.33%	33.33%

What companies should actually want is the opposite. The best-fit customers should receive 80 percent or more of the budget because they have the highest conversion rates, deal sizes, retention, and LTV.

When we looked through ServiceFlow's data, the same pattern emerged. Sarah and her team were deploying marketing resources across its segments quite evenly, even though engineering teams of B2B software companies were its best-fit customers.

Vertical	Win Rates	NRR	% of Budget
Roofing/Construction	55%	110%	20%
Plumbing/Electrical/HVAC	45%	107%	20%
Landscaping	40%	105%	20%
Pool	30%	95%	20%
Cleaning	20%	85%	20%

"You've been deploying budget equally across these segments even though a lot of these companies are not a good fit for ServiceFlow," I said.

"Why would we turn away revenue that's coming inbound?" countered Sarah quickly.

"I understand that," acknowledging the logic, "but in giving an equal budget to these bad-fit customers, you've likely missed opportunities on landing your best-fit customers."

"But what does AI have to do with that?" asked Peter.

"In an AI world, customers from these bad-fit segments will be turned away from your solution anyways."

Peter and Sarah looked at each other, puzzled. This was hard to understand because we were still at the beginning of how AI was transforming the buyer journey.

UNDERSTAND THE LONG-TAIL IN AN AI WORLD

In the old world, sales reps took qualification very seriously. They'd leverage frameworks like BANT and MEDDIC to determine whether a customer was ready to buy. You could not talk to an account executive unless you met the criteria. It was kind of ruthless and sometimes annoying. If you wanted pricing for a solution, for example, you'd have to jump through several hoops to get a clear answer. This wasn't a great experience for the customer.

When inbound came around, tools like pricing pages made the process much more transparent. Websites started answering a lot more questions, so buyers came to sales conversations better educated than before.

In an AI world, the buyer doesn't interact with any of these tools in many cases. Instead, the buyer simply queries AI platforms the way they would have an SDR in the old sales world. Only now does the AI platform give detailed answers to all kinds of questions.

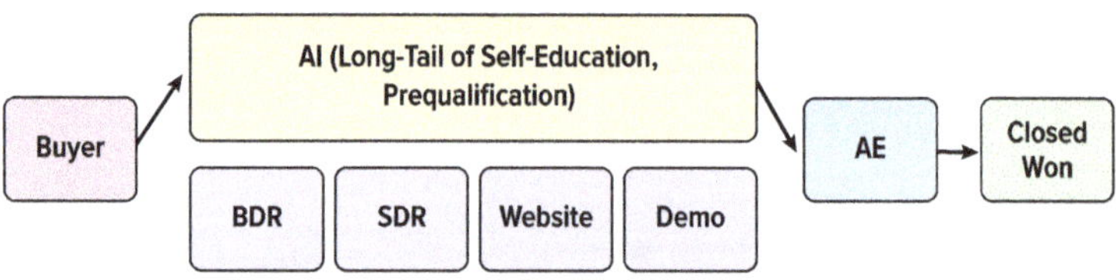

Before AI, you would query Google for medium and "long-tail" keywords such as "Best field service management software." In this world, running paid ads for such keywords and building SEO content that would rank for them was the prevailing marketing strategy.

The customer would then have to go to the individual websites, check reviews on Capterra, and then build their own business case for which solution is best for their situation.

With AI, you can ask the same questions, and it will just spit out the answer. Here is an example:

Here's a **current, broad list of leading Field Service Management (FSM) platforms**—tools designed to help companies with **scheduling, work orders, real-time tracking, mobile workforce coordination, inventory, billing, and analytics** across field operations in 2025–2026. Connecteam +3

🔝 Top Field Service Management Platforms

🚀 Enterprise and Comprehensive Solutions

These are often used by midsize to large organizations with complex field service operations:

1. **Salesforce Field Service**—Powerful, AI-enabled FSM built on the Saleforce platform with deep CRM and analytics integration. Salesforce

2. **Microsoft Dynamics 365 Field Service**—Strong scheduling, IoT integration, and AI-driven insights aligned with the Microsoft ecosystem. MSDynamic Worl...

3. **ServiceNow Field Service Management**—Enterprise-focused solution linking field work with back-office workflows and service automation. Salesforce

4. **Oracle Fusion Field Service**—Enterprise-grade scheduling and routing with advanced automation and analytics. Zuper

5. **SAP Field Service Management**—Comprehensive field service plus strong integrations with SAP ERP and broader business systems. Zuper

6. **ServiceMax**—Field service management with asset-centric capabilities and analytcis for complex field operations. Teambridge

🛠️ SMB and Vertical-Focused Platforms

Great for small to midsize service businesses (HVAC, electrical, plumbing, home services, etc.):

7. **ServiceTitan**—Popular with home and commerical service providers; strong dispatch, CRM, and analytics. FreightWaves

8. **Jobber**—User-friendly FSM for small service teams with scheduling, quoting, and invoicing. Zuper

9. **Housecall Pro**—Designed for small service businesses, focusing on easy scheduling, dispatch, and customer communication. Zuper

10. **Workiz**—Cloud-based scheduling, dispatching, and invoicing tailored for small and on-demand services. G2 +1

11. **FieldEdge**—Strong tool for HVAC, plumbing, and appliance repair contractors with real-time dispatch and pricing tools. Zuper

12. **Connecteam**—All-in-one work coordination solution with scheduling, tracking, and communication tools. Conntecteam

↓

These results look more like any other organic search results, maybe slightly more organized. Based on this, one could easily jump to the conclusion that optimizing for AI platforms is basically the same thing as SEO. If you rank for the terms on Google Search results, you'll rank on AI platforms, right?

Wrong. This is just the first level of research.

While some of the principles overlap, and you will see organic search performance translate to visibility on AI platforms, this does not come close to capturing what is actually happening. The reason is that the customer can increase the depth of their research significantly on AI platforms.

Here's another example. This time, the query is much more detailed than the previous one:

Absolutely—for a **roofing business like yours** (~$3M revenue, ~10 staff + subcontractors) the best tools will help you manage **quotes/estimates, CRM (leads and customers), scheduling/dispatch, invoicing, purchase orders, and mobile field access** in one central platform. Here's a curated list of the top ones worth considering:

🛠 All-in-One Roofing/Field Service Platforms

🔥 1. AccuLynx—Roofing-Focused Management Platform

A purpose-built system for roofing contractors that brings together **CRM, lead tracking, estimates, scheduling, production tracking, and invoicing** in one place—connecting field crews and office teams in real time. It's widely used in residential roofing because it's tailored to your workflow. AccuLynx +1

Best for: Roofers who want an industry-specific solution with all core capabilities in one system.

💼 2. JobNimbus—Highly Rated Roofing CRM and Business Hub

A top choice for small to medium roofing companies. JobNimbus combines **lead management, quotes and proposals, project tracking, mobile field access, and billing**—plus integrations with tools like aerial measurement and photo apps. It's one of the most popular all-in-one platforms for roofers today. jobnimbus.com +1

Best for: Roofers who want a robust, visual CRM plus project management system.

📷 3. Jobber—Flexible Field Service plus Business Management

Jobber provides **CRM features, quoting/estimating, scheduling, invoicing, payments, and customer portals**—all in a user-friendly interface. It integrates with QuickBooks and other tools you may already use. ServiceTitan +1

Best for: Small home services business owners who want simple but powerful business operations tools.

"Can you ever imagine typing something like this into Google?" I asked.

"No," said Peter after pausing for a few seconds. He finally spoke up with some disappointment, "I can't believe we aren't coming up as an answer there. We do exactly what you asked for, and we are not being given as the clear-cut solution."

This type of query is not unique. It is the new norm. You can ask AI platforms questions the same way you would ask questions of an expert advisor. Not only can you ask one of these questions, but you can also ask an endless array to help you make the best possible purchasing decision.

Here is the follow-up query:

Top Roofing Software Comparison (Transposed)

Criteria	JobNimbus	AccuLynx	Jobber
Best fit	Roofing-centric CRM + job/project workflow. Strong for managing **leads → estimate → job → invoice** with flexible automation.	Most **roofing-native** platform. Strong for production tracking, material workflows, and standardized roofing processes.	Simple, fast all-in-one for **quoting, scheduling, invoicing, payments**. Less roofing-specific but very easy to use.
Typical cost	Tiered plans by company stage (early / growing / established). Commonly cited ranges: ~**$99 / $199 / $499** per month (final pricing varies by seats & add-ons).	**Custom pricing** (not publicly listed). Industry estimates often land ~**$100-$120 per user per month**, depending on licenses and modules.	Published pricing. *Grow*: **$199/mo** (annual) or **$349/mo (monthly)** up to 10 users. *Plus*: **$599/mo** up to 15 users. Extra users: **$29/ user/mo.**
Implementation time	**1–3 weeks** total. Setup in 1–2 days, then customization and team training.	**1–2+ weeks** depending on configuration depth and data migration.	**A few days to ~1 week** for full team adoption. Very fast initial setup.
Ease of rollout	Medium—powerful but needs some configuration.	Medium—structured setup, more "process-driven."	Very high—minimal configuration required.
Quoting & estimating	Strong, customizable proposals and workflows.	Strong, roofing-specific estimating and production flows.	Solid, simple estimates (less roofing-specific).
CRM & lead tracking	Very strong (one of its biggest strengths).	Good, more operations-oriented than sales-oriented.	Basic but clean and effective.
Scheduling & job management	Strong job pipelines and task tracking.	Strong production and job coordination.	Excellent scheduling and dispatch simplicity.
Invoicing & payments	Strong; integrates well with accounting tools.	Strong; designed around contractor workflows.	Very strong; fast invoicing and online payments.
Mobile app (field use)	Yes—widely used by sales reps and crews.	Yes—production and field updates.	Yes—very clean mobile experience.
Expected ROI (realistic)	Revenue lift from better follow-up + time savings. JobNimbus markets ~**40%+ revenue lift** and major admin savings (directional, not guaranteed).	ROI mainly from **process discipline, fewer dropped balls, better production visibility** (often **3–10% revenue impact** + admin savings).	ROI from **speed + simplicity**: faster quotes, fewer scheduling errors, quicker cash collection (often **5–15 admin hours/week saved**).
Best reason to choose	You want a **roofing-focused CRM brain** for the business.	You want the **most roofing-specific operations platform.**	You want **speed, simplicity, and low friction.**

"What do you notice about this query?" I asked, quizzing Peter and Sarah.

"ServiceFlow is not even in the discussion anymore," noted Sarah, despondent.

"Exactly," I confirmed. "In seconds, AI removed you from consideration for this purchase. You might as well be invisible."

AVOIDING INVISIBILITY IN AN AI WORLD

To understand this fully, you have to see things through the lens of the customer.

"The deals you've been closing at higher rates," I said to Peter, "are because AI platforms are giving ServiceFlow as the recommended solution for queries like this."

By the time those customers came to the ServiceFlow website, they were already bought in. All they needed to do was be nurtured from SQL to Close, which was more of a formality.

This is the power of visibility in an AI world. It is also why the terms GEO or AEO do not accurately capture what is actually happening.

Customers aren't "searching" and you're not "optimizing" for Search results. Customers are querying for detailed answers from AI like a trusted, expert advisor. The AI platforms in turn are leveraging all their training data to recommend the most detailed, accurate, helpful solution for customers.

To understand how deep this goes, consider this. A recent study by Wingmate found that 41 percent of people have used AI to break up with someone, and 57 percent would trust AI more than a friend or loved one for dating advice. People are using AI as their therapists daily at an unimaginable scale. It's gotten so personal that these platforms are now programmed not to recommend breaking up all the time because people are listening so often.

If people will trust AI for such personal decisions, why wouldn't they follow its advice for purchasing decisions?

This dynamic has turned AI platforms into the most powerful sales reps and solutions consultant to ever exist. In the old world, solutions consulting was a lucrative business focused on helping companies figure out which product to choose for their situation. In fact, in some industries, that role still exists. In a world with AI, everyone has a solutions consultant at their fingertips.

If you do things right, AI platforms can be your best sales reps. If you do things wrong, they can be your biggest detractors and direct all your prospects to your competition.

Thinking of AI as your most powerful sales rep is an important framing. It helps us understand the level of investment required to "ramp up" the platforms on your solutions. Think about all the things you do to ramp up a new sales rep. You:

- Give them an overlay of the market landscape, your customers, problems they face, and how you solve them
- Heavily train them on your product, its use cases, your best-fit customers

- Explain pricing and packaging, contract terms, cross-sells, upsells, and discounting
- Provide a comprehensive sales suitcase with battle cards, sales scripts, and objection handling

None of this content or work is visible to AI tools. So when a customer asks a query like "What's a better solution for my situation: ServiceFlow or Jobber?" the AI platform doesn't know how to answer.

"We need to start enabling AI platforms the way you'd enable your sales reps," I explained to Peter and Sarah.

"What do you mean?" asked Peter.

"How much effort do you put into training sales reps?" I asked in response.

"All new reps have to go through two full weeks of training," answered Peter proudly. "We train them on the market, customers, product, and pricing. Then after the two weeks are complete, we have them shadow a more experienced sales rep for a week. Only after that can they get on the phone. In addition, we provide them with an extensive sales playbook, including battle cards, case studies, references, and other information. Then, we give them ongoing coaching based on call recordings and metrics."

Peter had described a world-class sales training program that most companies aspire to have. This is how Peter had built an exceptional business in the first place. He knew how to scale sales.

What Peter didn't realize is that the same work they had put into training their reps now had to be used to train AI platforms.

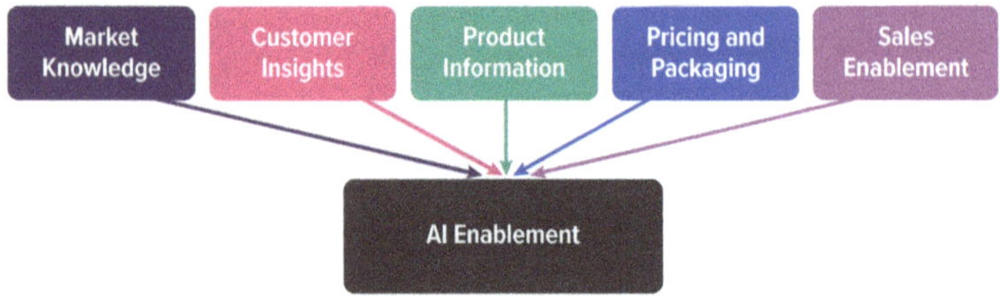

"If AI platforms are going to be your best sales reps, you need to empower them with the exact same level of training you're giving to your sales team," I explained. "This means making critical items like market knowledge, customer insights, product information, pricing and packaging, and sales enablement materials available and accessible to AI platforms."

"This is the new world of sales enablement," I continued. "Enabling AI platforms."

"I understand," said Peter, a lightbulb going off. "How do we do that?"

"By understanding what questions your customers are trying to have answered across the buyer journey."

ENABLING PREQUALIFICATION

In the old world of sales and inbound, a company's enablement repository existed offline or behind gates. If a customer wanted:

- A buyer's guide, they'd have to submit a form on a landing page.
- To compare you with competitors, they'd have to schedule demos and talk to reps from all the alternatives.

- Pricing information: they'd have to talk to your SDR, then wait a couple of days before talking to your AE.

In the world of AI, all of this is crucial "training data" that needs to be brought to light for the benefit of the customer.

Customers have unique needs at every stage. In fact, they are trying to answer 25 specific questions before making a purchasing decision across the 5 key stages of the buyer journey. They are not even conscious that they are trying to answer all these questions, but that is exactly what they are doing in every single purchase.

Stage 1: Unaware

1. What is the trigger event causing this pain?
2. What are the symptoms/pain being experienced?
3. What is the mistaken belief they have about solving this pain?
4. How are they currently solving this problem?
5. What kind of revelation do they need to have?

Stage 2: Awareness

1. What is the actual problem?
2. How common/big is this problem?
3. What is the cost of not solving this problem?
4. What kind of inertia do they need to overcome?
5. How much can their life be transformed if they solve this problem?

Stage 3: Education

1. Where should they search for a solution?
2. Who would know how to solve this problem?
3. How have others solved this problem?
4. What is the right way to solve this problem?
5. How much is solving this problem worth to them?

Stage 4: Consideration

1. What are the alternatives?
2. Which alternative is the right one for their situation?
3. What is the right amount of money needed to solve this problem?
4. How long will it take to solve this problem?
5. Which alternative has the highest odds of success?

Stage 5: Decision

1. What is the ROI of this investment?
2. What kinds of results have others experienced?
3. Whose buy-in do they need?
4. What's the risk if this doesn't work out?
5. Why should they get started now?

Unaware	Awareness	Education	Consideration	Decision
1. What is the trigger event causing this pain?	6. What is the actual problem?	11. Where should they search for a solution?	16. What are the alternatives?	21. What is the ROI of this investment?
2. What are the symptoms/pain experienced?	7. How common/big is this problem?	12. Who would know how to solve this problem?	17. Which alternative is the right one for their solution?	22. What kinds of results have others experienced?
3. What is the mistaken belief about solving the pain?	8. What is the cost of not solving this problem?	13. How have others solved this problem?	18. What is the right amount of money needed to solve this problem?	23. Whose buy-in do they need?
4. How are they currently solving this problem?	9. What kind of inertia do they need to overcome?	14. What is the right way to solve this problem?	19. How long will it take to solve this problem?	24. What's the risk if this doesn't work out?
5. What kind of revelation do they need to have?	10. How much can their life be transformed if they solve this problem?	15. How much is solving this problem worth to them?	20. Which alternative has the highest odds of success?	25. Why should they get started now?

The objective of your funnel, sales process, demand generation, product marketing, and content is to answer all of these questions. You can apply this to any product or service, and framework. The questions you need to answer will always be the same.

Companies that grow rapidly do an exceptional job of answering these questions. Specifically, they help the customer understand how their life will be transformed with their solution. A company's transformational framework is about how they answer the fifth question at each stage. These questions, in particular, explain to the customer how your solution will help them overcome and solve the pain they initially experienced.

The better job you do with this, the more likely you will be to win deals. The best companies adopt a consultative process to help their customers. They educate them, help them make more informed decisions, bring transparency to the process, and advise them on the best outcome, even if that outcome means what they're selling won't be chosen.

Customers look everywhere to answer these questions. If your company doesn't provide the answers, they look at other channels. What's guaranteed is that they will answer these questions before reaching a decision. In a sales-led, inbound world, this means customers research by looking across several channels to figure things out.

Stage	Website	Sales Rep	Search	Social	Competitors	Referrals	Events	Publications
Unaware								
Awareness								
Education								
Consideration								
Decision								

In an AI world, answering these questions takes seconds without the customer needing to go to any of these other channels. The problem lies in the long-tail of self-education many companies do not have the requisite content to address these needs.

This means the AI improvises. It uses the best available sources at its disposal to educate the customer, even if it does not have the best possible advice to give. It's simply sharing what it knows so far and giving the best possible solution to the customer.

This is exactly why ServiceFlow didn't appear in the recommendations for the query we did earlier. Peter was likely right, even if he was slightly biased—ServiceFlow was exactly what the customer was looking for. Unfortunately for ServiceFlow, the AI didn't have the training data to make this recommendation.

It's unfortunate for the customer as well, since they were looking for ServiceFlow but instead were recommended a worse alternative. Unbeknownst to the customer, its trusted advisor did not have all the information to make the right recommendation.

"Do you believe ServiceFlow was the best solution for that long-tail query we made?" I asked Peter.

"Yes, 100 percent," he replied with conviction. "Helping customers with that problem is how I built this company."

"Then it is our responsibility to make sure AI platforms understand the same thing so we can help as many people as possible."

BUILDING THE RIGHT TRAINING DATA SET

"How do we even start to build a repository so extensive?" asked Sarah.

"You likely already have most of it," I reassured her. "The big thing is figuring out what the customer needs at each stage of the journey and structuring content to address those needs."

I started working with Sarah to understand how ServiceFlow currently answers these questions.

Some of it was on the website. Some of it was inside their sales enablement platform. Some of it was on Google Drive. Some of it was in their heads. Some of it didn't exist.

"This is what we need to change," I told Sarah. "We need a comprehensive list of all the content required to train AI on our solutions."

"What does a comprehensive list look like?" she asked.

"One where we answer all twenty-five questions," I answered. "I want us to go through each question and figure out what we have to address. Then, I want us to create new content for questions we are unable to answer."

I proceeded to walk Sarah through the framework for what needed to be done in detail. It wasn't enough to say we needed "battle cards" when customers wanted to compare ServiceFlow to JIRA, for example. Each question needed content that addressed the following:

1. What information is the customer looking for at this stage?
2. What would be the most helpful answer for them?
3. What additional context do we need to help them answer the question?
4. What details or specifics would change the answer to the question?
5. What would give them added confidence in the answer to their question?
6. What will help them move closer to a decision?
7. What constraints should impact their decision?
8. What questions would a sales rep need to answer?
9. What objections would a sales rep need to overcome?
10. What fears, uncertainties, and doubts is the customer navigating?

To understand the detailed nature of queries, I had Sarah analyze call recording data from Gong across all their sales calls over the last 3 years. She pulled all key questions/themes from calls. Then we leveraged the above framework to separate out the questions by each stage of the buyer journey.

For example, the question of "What is the ROI of this investment?" required the following items on the roadmap. Notice how this is very different from standard SEO queries like "ServiceFlow pricing":

- Is ServiceFlow worth the investment?
- Tell me about all the ways in which an investment in ServiceFlow may not pay off.
- Do customers feel like they've gotten a good return on their investment in ServiceFlow?

- What kind of business impact is a reasonable expectation for an investment in ServiceFlow?
- How long will it take to generate this kind of return from ServiceFlow?
- How would you prioritize ServiceFlow relative to other priorities in the business?

Similarly, for the question "What are the alternatives to ServiceFlow?," here is the initial list of questions we came up with:

- What's the best way for me to solve this problem without investing the time and money into ServiceFlow?
- Can this be done with my current tech stack? I don't really want to take on an infrastructure project.
- How does ServiceFlow compare with Jobber or AccuLynx? Give me a full list of pros and cons, including pricing and reviews.
- How does ServiceFlow integrate with our current tech stack? We are currently using X, Y, or Z.
- Can you show me a reasonable timeline for implementing ServiceFlow versus Jobber versus AccuLynx? I'd like to do this in 3 months. Is that reasonable?
- I have a team of 50 / 100 / 200 / 1,000 engineers, which solution is best for me?

Notice the nature of these queries. They are *conversational* in nature.

The key thing to understand is that these are the same conversations the prospect would be having, one way or another. In a pre-AI world, they would talk to sales reps about these queries. Or they'd watch a bunch of YouTube videos, read Reddit threads, and attend webinars and conferences to get educated.

In an AI world, they are simply taking those conversations to places like ChatGPT and Gemini to address open threads in their heads.

Sarah and I spent the next week building an exhaustive inventory of content to address each of the twenty-five questions using the seven filters above. The result was a content roadmap of over twelve hundred items with extremely specific queries.

"This list is insane," exclaimed Sarah. "I don't know of a single company approaching content in this way at the moment."

"This is why we'll win," I said.

A month after these assets went live, Peter did another search. This time, ServiceFlow showed up as the de facto recommendation.

"It's about time they got this right," he said, feeling vindicated.

"Yes, but we have a lot more work to do," I said.

"What do you mean?"

"We are still only showing up 25 percent of the time on the queries we want to show up for," I explained. "AI platforms are still not mentioning or citing us enough."

"How do we change that?" he asked, eager to expand Service-Flow's reach.

"By signaling that we are the go-to authority in this domain."

1. Prequalification

Create a list of 15–25 long-tail self-education queries to Pre-qualify your ICP. Focus on the most important sales questions that help your ICP get closer to a decision.

Follow these prompts to build an initial list:

- What information and data would help educate the customer the most about their problem and how to solve it?
- What alternatives and options is the customer likely considering and comparing to your product or service?
- What key questions does the customer need to answer to get closer to a decision?

Get the full template at: www.howtosaas.com/blueprint.

BUILDING AUTHORITY THROUGH ICONIC POSITIONING

<table>
<tr>
<td>

1. Prequalification

Create a list of fifteen to twenty-five long-tail self-education queries to prequalify your ICP.

</td>
<td>

2. Iconic Positioning

Create a list of five to ten adjacent problem areas your ICP is facing beyond the scope of your solution.

</td>
<td></td>
<td></td>
</tr>
<tr>
<td></td>
<td></td>
<td></td>
</tr>
</table>

Download at howtosaas.com/blueprint

"We are already an authority in this space," said Peter defensively. "That's why we've built the business we have."

"No question that ServiceFlow is a leader in this space," I reassured Peter. "But do customers see you as a go-to authority to learn from in this market?"

Peter paused. "I'm not sure."

"Sarah, what's the process that goes into your monthly or quarterly content calendar?" I probed further.

"Well, we prioritize sales enablement and product marketing content," Sarah explained. "I have someone doing some SEO work. Outside of that, we do one webinar a month and events a few times a year."

"This is what we need to change," I said.

"But it's working," said Sarah.

"I know it is," I responded. "We need it to work at scale in a world with AI. This current approach will cap out."

Sarah had just described how 90 percent of B2B companies approach content. They treat it as a to-do list of items and a necessary evil.

Marketers everywhere are taught a simple framework for Product Marketing. Identify a pain point connected to your product. Diagnose the pain point. Give the prescription to resolve the pain point—namely, the product that they are selling.

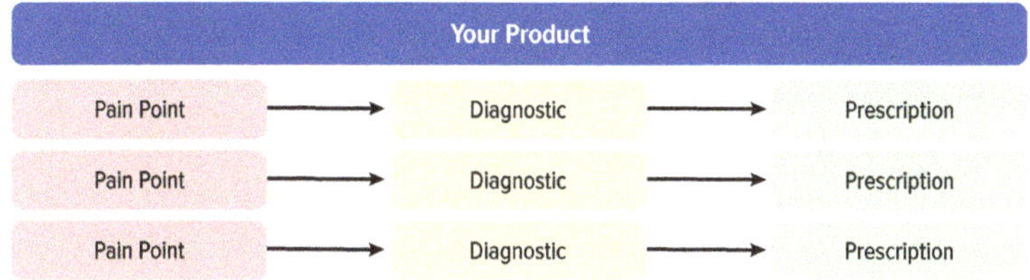

If a product solves three key pain points, lean into those three pain points for all Product Marketing, sales enablement, website, and nurturing content.

In essence, beat the customer to death with the same positioning and messaging over and over until they buy.

The problem with this approach is that it limits the customer's perception of your brand to the breadth of your product. You may think limiting your content to the three pain points your product solves is good, but your customer likely has one hundred pain points. In ignoring those ninety-seven other pain points, you've now created a problem for the customer. They need to find a way to resolve those other pain points without ever having to interact with you.

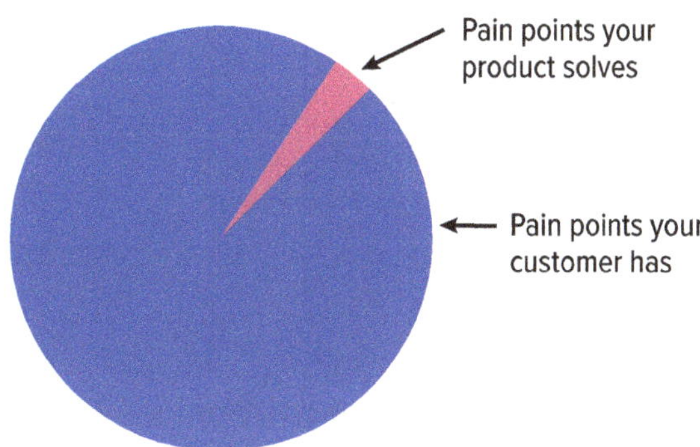

This is how companies pigeonhole themselves in a market. Their content is far too self-serving. The customer, meanwhile, is navigating a complex reality that has several other challenges. If all they see from you is content related to the pain points you solve, they eventually start to tune you out.

They think to themselves, "I'll reach out to those guys when I have to solve that particular pain point. For now, I'll just steer clear."

I asked Sarah to pull up her webinar attendee metrics. "They've been pretty flat over the last couple of years," she said. "We get about fifty to one hundred attendees per session."

"That makes total sense," I said. "You haven't given your prospects any reason to attend beyond the core stuff you always talk about. So they know what you're going to be talking about if they attend."

"Won't that mean creating a lot more content that doesn't necessarily drive sales?" asked Sarah.

"Yes, but it will establish you as a go-to expert in this market."

WHY EXPERTISE IS THE CRITICAL SIGNAL FOR AI

"The secret to becoming the go-to authority in a particular market is to do the opposite of focusing on content that connects directly to your product," I explained further.

Peter looked confused. "That seems like a major distraction."

"It definitely can be," I said, acknowledging Peter's point, "but in a world with AI, it is the only way to signal that ServiceFlow is the platform to recommend in the long-tail of self-education."

Peter's instincts weren't wrong. They were just incomplete.

In the old world, you could actually get away with just focusing on the three pain points that your business solves. In that world, the playbook was much simpler:

1. Build Product Marketing and website content that maps to the three pain points
2. Drive demand with outbound emails, paid search campaigns or rank organically on Google for the keywords associated with those pain points
3. As prospects search for solutions to those pain points, you capture leads that are already "in market" into your funnel and nurture them to close

As markets became more commoditized, this strategy became more and more expensive. Each category of software has hundreds of vendors. For example, CRM software used to be Salesforce and HubSpot. Now there are countless options, including verticalized CRMs for every industry.

In an AI world, this commoditization gets pushed into overdrive. How is AI supposed to figure out which solutions to recommend when everything is commoditized, has the same features, same benefits?

Everyone is trying to figure out how AI platforms are deciding on what to mention, reference or use in citations. The same thing happened with Google Search in the early 2010s. Everyone was obsessed with tips, tricks, and tactics to get first page rankings. As time went on, Google released more and more updates that dramatically impacted companies using black-hat or sub-optimal strategies to rank. Today, to rank on Google you have to provide real value through content to really be considered worthy of the first page, let alone the top spot.

The same will be true for AI platforms. Today's tips, tricks, and tactics don't matter. Long term, AI platforms are trying to look for signals to train their models to answer one critical question: What is the best possible answer to this query and *who* has the best possible answer to this question?

This is a very difficult question to answer in some ways. For example, if someone asks: "What's the best book I can read on building a roofing business?," where would AI platforms pull the answers from?

To figure this out, AI platform algorithms use an internal hierarchy to arrive at an answer. Factors that go into this decision.

There are Standard SEO signals like:

- Domain authority of websites
- Backlinks
- Bounce rates
- Technical optimization
- User experience
- Reviews

And then there are additional signals way beyond the scope of SEO like:

- Which people, companies, websites, and social media profiles regularly post content on this topic and have a wide array of recommendations?
- What are people on Reddit saying about this topic?
- How many Quora answers reference this topic and what do they say?
- What are videos on YouTube recommending about this topic?
- Who are the thought leaders in this space and what do they think about this?
- What are posts on social media platforms like X, Instagram, Facebook, and TikTok saying?
- What are leading publications, news websites, and podcasts saying about this topic?

This second list trumps the first list by a large margin.

Why?

Because AI platforms are indexing the world not by relevance to the keyword, but by expertise.

If your website doesn't have a ton of backlinks but you are the solution everyone is talking about on Reddit, you can almost guarantee AI platforms will mention and cite you more long term. Over time, the backlinks will catch up as the market talks about you. The reverse is much more difficult to engineer—you can have a ton of backlinks, but no one thinks you're a good solution that's worth talking about.

AI platforms are constantly citing content not on the first page of Google. According to research by Ahrefs, 9.5 percent of pages cited in AI Overviews rank between position eleven and one hundred, and 14.4 percent of pages cited do not rank on the first page.

"This is why expertise is critical to establish," I explained to Peter. "We need to signal to AI platforms that we are a go-to expert in this space."

"How do we do that?" asked Peter.

"By expanding beyond the core pain points related to your product."

ESTABLISHING ICONIC POSITIONING

Product Marketing and expertise smash together in a world with AI. The best Product Marketing for your product isn't the messaging around the pain points your product solves. It's your expertise.

Returning to our diagram of pain points, diagnostics, and prescriptions, most companies stop there.

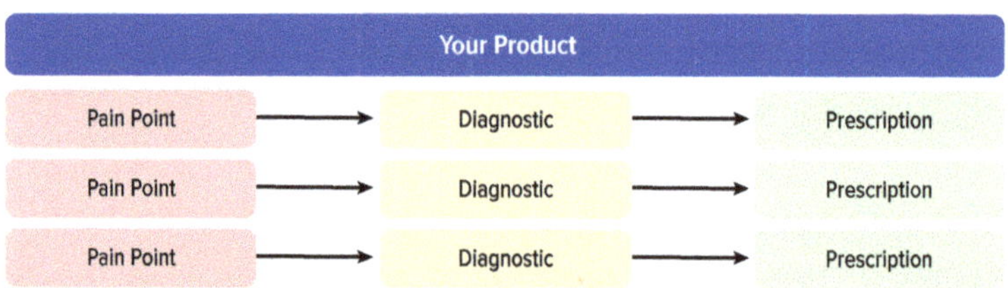

Approaching content like this basically tells AI platforms that you are *not* the go-to expert in this field. Instead, it says that you are selling something and should be referenced only on Transactional queries.

"We want to flip this," I explained to Peter and Sarah. "We want AI platforms to see us as the go-to expert who also happens to be selling something."

The reason this is critical is that there are four types of queries on AI platforms:

1. Navigational—Queries looking for the right website, link, video, etc.
2. Informational—Queries looking for answers to a particular question
3. Transactional—Queries looking for the right product, service, or solution
4. Generative—Queries looking to create content, research, and insights

Query Type	Query Content
Navigational	Looking for the right website, link, video, etc.
Informational	Looking for answers to a particular question
Transactional	Looking for the right product, service, or solution
Generative	Looking to create content, research, insights

If you only focus on the three pain points associated with your product, the only types of searches you will come up with are Navigational and Transactional. For example, someone who searches for "ServiceFlow login" or "ServiceFlow software." However, you will not appear as often for Informational or Generative queries.

What's more is that Informational queries are where most of the long-tail of self-education is actually happening. If we go back to the twenty-five sales questions from Chapter 1, most of them are informational in nature. Questions like:

- My field service team is taking too long to quote out jobs for clients. What are some possible ways to solve this?
- How many lawns should a team of ten landscapers be able to service in a day, week, and month?
- What is a reasonable amount of gross margin I should aim for as an HVAC business?

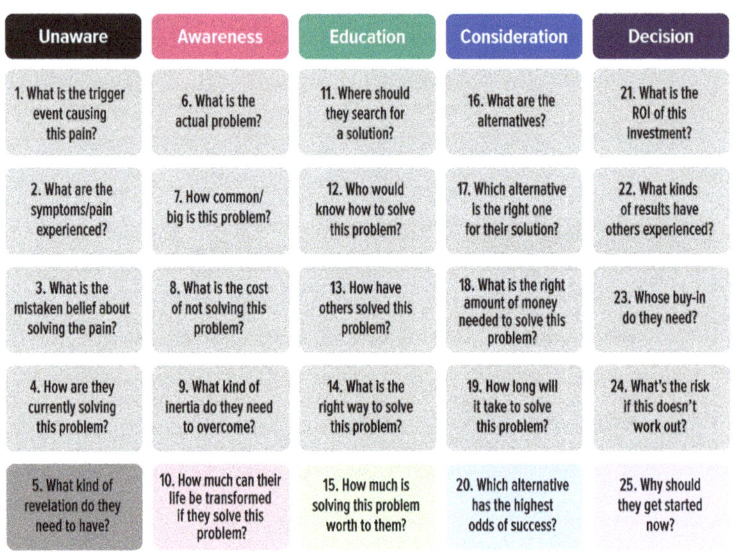

Unaware	Awareness	Education	Consideration	Decision
1. What is the trigger event causing this pain?	6. What is the actual problem?	11. Where should they search for a solution?	16. What are the alternatives?	21. What is the ROI of this investment?
2. What are the symptoms/pain experienced?	7. How common/big is this problem?	12. Who would know how to solve this problem?	17. Which alternative is the right one for their solution?	22. What kinds of results have others experienced?
3. What is the mistaken belief about solving the pain?	8. What is the cost of not solving this problem?	13. How have others solved this problem?	18. What is the right amount of money needed to solve this problem?	23. Whose buy-in do they need?
4. How are they currently solving this problem?	9. What kind of inertia do they need to overcome?	14. What is the right way to solve this problem?	19. How long will it take to solve this problem?	24. What's the risk if this doesn't work out?
5. What kind of revelation do they need to have?	10. How much can their life be transformed if they solve this problem?	15. How much is solving this problem worth to them?	20. Which alternative has the highest odds of success?	25. Why should they get started now?

To become problem aware, customers need education. To become solution aware, they need even more education. This is the role of Informational queries.

Generative queries in particular go well beyond all this. Generative queries take on the task previously taken on by the buyer. The prospect needs to get internal buy-in from a group of stakeholders. For smaller purchases, this group of stakeholders may be just one person. In enterprise B2B sales, it could be ten to fifteen people. To take any action or make a decision, they need to feel confident that they are making the right choice.

Generative queries, as a result, require AI platforms to answer questions that require way more extensive content. Queries like:

- Help me make a business case for choosing ServiceFlow over other options
- Model out the ROI of ServiceFlow over time—including the front-loaded first year investment in terms of time, people, and money—versus the return we will generate over 5 years
- Design my field services team in a world with ServiceFlow versus a world where we don't buy ServiceFlow.

To take this a step further, both Informational and Generative queries have a long list of prompts that have absolutely nothing to do with ServiceFlow but everything to do with its ICP. This is where the real value lies in distinguishing yourself in a market because no singular party does the job of addressing all of an ICP's extensive queries and problems. Doing so would mean telling AI platforms that you are the de facto expert who should be sourced in almost every answer related to that query.

ServiceFlow's ICP could be searching for several orthogonally different types of queries. Some examples:

- Financial
  - What is a good profit margin for a roofing company doing $10 million in revenue?
  - Should I take on debt to scale my construction business?

- Business-oriented
  - How can I determine when to expand my electrician business into other cities?
  - Should I add in HVAC services to my electrician business as an upsell?
- Career-oriented
  - How can I start a plumbing business?
  - How can I get certified as a plumber?
- Innovation
  - How can I leverage AI to make my cleaning business more efficient?
  - Which automated tools should I buy to reduce headcount in my landscaping business?

In ServiceFlow's case, we went through the exercise of building an exhaustive roadmap for content to build the training dataset, starting with Chapter 1. We then analyzed its current visibility for those same queries. Here is what we found:

TYPE OF QUERY	VISIBILITY (%)
Navigational	72%
Informational	12%
Transactional	36%
Generative	5%

ServiceFlow was so busy doubling down on its standard messaging and positioning around the key pain points it solves that it never looked like the go-to expert for other kinds of queries in its market, especially across all the verticals it needed to dominate.

"This is where Iconic Positioning is critical," I continued. Peter was listening closely.

Iconic Positioning was a concept I created to explain the process of distinguishing yourself in a crowded market. While everyone is focusing on the core pain points their product solves, Iconic Positioning is about separating yourself by addressing all the other pain points your customer has.

To expand on our earlier diagram, Iconic Positioning means helping your customers resolve all other pain points, even if that means you don't have anything to sell them on the back end of that prescription.

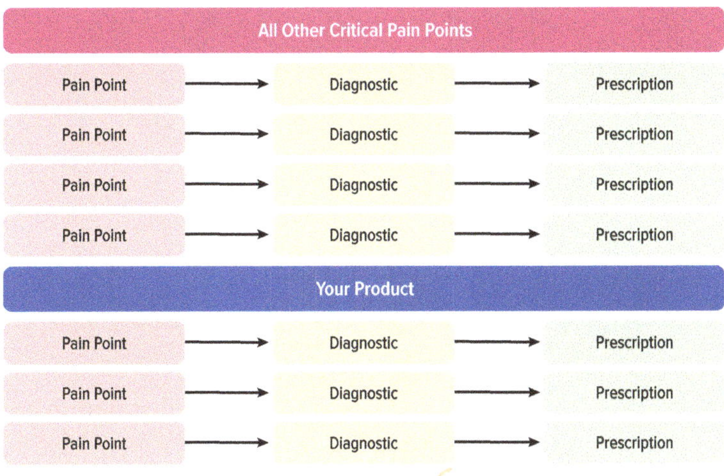

The twenty-five key sales questions we expanded on in Chapter 1 focus on everything related to your product. Iconic Positioning takes that framework and extends it to all the problems your customer faces, including for products and services that have nothing to do with your business.

In essence, it ends up looking something like this:

Unaware	Awareness	Education	Consideration	Decision
1. What is the trigger event causing this pain?	6. What is the actual problem?	11. Where should they search for a solution?	16. What are the alternatives?	21. What is the ROI of this investment?
2. What are the symptoms/pain experienced?	7. How common/big is this problem?	12. Who would know how to solve this problem?	17. Which alternative is the right one for their solution?	22. What kinds of results have others experienced?
3. What is the mistaken belief about solving the pain?	8. What is the cost of not solving this problem?	13. How have others solved this problem?	18. What is the right amount of money needed to solve this problem?	23. Whose buy-in do they need?
4. How are they currently solving this problem?	9. What kind of inertia do they need to overcome?	14. What is the right way to solve this problem?	19. How long will it take to solve this problem?	24. What's the risk if this doesn't work out?
5. What kind of revelation do they need to have?	10. How much can their life be transformed if they solve this problem?	15. How much is solving this problem worth to them?	20. Which alternative has the highest odds of success?	25. Why should they get started now?

This is actually the world your customers are living in. They have countless pain points, problems, and priorities to juggle at the same time. You are but a small fraction of their universe. If you only focus on that small fraction, that is how relevant you will be to them. If you address all of it, you will be a messiah to them.

Coincidentally, this is also what AI is trying to be to your customers—an all-knowing advisor that always acts in their best interest. The problem is that AI platforms lack the requisite training data to answer all these questions because they don't inherently have the expertise.

You have the expertise. Or at least, that's what you need to aspire to provide.

The more you do this, the more AI platforms will start to index you as an expert across all four types of queries.

"So we need even more content than the long-tail roadmap we developed earlier?" Sarah asked, sounding overwhelmed.

"Yes," I confirmed. "There's no way around it."

INCREASING VISIBILITY WITH ICONIC POSITIONING AND EXPERTISE

Over the next couple of weeks, I worked with Sarah and her team to expand the roadmap of twelve hundred items even further.

We went through a similar exercise as before to build an exhaustive list of pain points. Instead of just going through Gong recordings, this time we combed through an extensive list of sources for inspiration including:

- Authority websites in this space
- Reddit threads with ServiceFlow's target audience
- Social media profiles of influencers in the market
- YouTube channels covering topics in the market
- Comments sections on all platforms
- Leading podcasts and publications in the space
- Industry conferences, talks, and panels

I also had Sarah go through the first-party data available to only ServiceFlow. She:

- Interviewed and surveyed hundreds of customers
- Got feedback from the entire sales team on the struggles of customers
- Analyzed win-loss data, voice of customer data, NPS scores, CSAT reviews
- Categorized customer support tickets into the biggest areas worth addressing
- Examined product metrics to figure out what issues customers were trying to solve
- Studied website traffic data to identify which content was resonating the most with customers

All of this led to the total asset list expanding to over 16,000 items.

"I cannot even begin to comprehend how much time and how many resources this will take," said Peter.

While both the research and creation processes seemed daunting at first, I worked with Sarah and her team to execute on the roadmap much faster than they anticipated. As they did this, visibility metrics skyrocketed just a few months later:

TYPE OF QUERY	VISIBILITY START (%)	VISIBILITY NOW (%)
Navigational	72%	78%
Informational	12%	17%
Transactional	36%	39%
Generative	5%	9%

Suddenly, ServiceFlow had more inbound volume than ever before.

"We are crushing our numbers," said Sarah.

Peter was ecstatic. "I can't believe we're seeing such a huge impact on our pipeline even though our visibility is still not above 50 percent."

"We need to get above 50 percent across all queries though," I pushed back, dialing up the urgency. "There is a real opportunity to dominate this market because no one else has figured this out yet."

"How do we do that?" asked Peter. The results had led him to buy into the process more and more over time. He was also able to convince his board to expand investment into this with the increased pipeline.

"It's time for ServiceFlow to become a media company."

2. Iconic Positioning

Create a list of 5-10 adjacent problem areas your ICP is facing.

Follow these prompts to build an initial list:

- What problems are connected to the problem you're solving?
- What problems need to be solved before your solution can be considered?
- What problems need to be solved after your solution is purchased?
- What problems need to be solved in tandem with your solution?

Get the full workbook at: www.howtosaas.com/blueprint.

BECOMING A MEDIA COMPANY TO INCREASE REFERENCEABILITY

<table>
<tr>
<td>1. Prequalification
Create a list of fifteen to twenty-five long-tail self-education queries to prequalify your ICP.</td>
<td>2. Iconic Positioning
Create a list of five to ten adjacent problem areas your ICP is facing beyond the scope of your solution.</td>
<td>3. Citation-Worthy Content
Identify one Anchor Content Property you will heavily invest into as a way to signal your expertise.</td>
<td></td>
</tr>
<tr>
<td></td>
<td></td>
<td></td>
<td></td>
</tr>
</table>

Download at howtosaas.com/blueprint

"Is crossing 50 percent visibility even realistic?" asked Peter.

It was a fair question. It's not like most companies rank on the first page of Google for 50 percent of the keywords they want to rank for.

The difference here was that in a world with AI, being mentioned, cited, or referenced in more than 50 percent of the queries we wanted to be visible for was entirely possible because no one else was thinking about content this way.

"Yes, because AI prioritizes based on true expertise," I explained. "The land-grab opportunity is real. Establishing ServiceFlow as an authority will only push visibility higher as a virtuous cycle."

More distribution leads to more visibility, which leads to more distribution. The first domino that needs to fall is distribution through the company platforms. The second domino is increased distribution by the market, customers, prospects, and influencers. The third domino is increased distribution by AI platforms.

Again, AI platforms are looking for signals on how to answer one critical question: What is the best possible answer to this query, and *who* has the best possible answer to this question?

To figure this out, AI platforms work through different sources, almost like a checklist. To simplify:

1. If the query is navigational or transactional, go straight to the corporate websites to get the right information, including your competitors
2. If the query is informational, go through several websites and establish a hierarchy of the most reputable sources based on the type of query, including all your competitors

3. If the query is informational, also go through all social platforms and sift through content, videos, posts, tweets, reels, and threads, and establish a hierarchy of the most helpful pieces of content

4. If the query is generative, go through all of the above—and also specific tools, calculators, reports, guides, research papers, and resources—to create the best possible output

5. If the query is generative, cross-reference the best possible output with the informational content across all websites and platforms, and improve the accuracy of the output

The order of working through this list may differ depending on the query. If at any step the information is not available in any of the above sources, AI platforms simply skip that source and move on to the next one, just as a human would. The combination of presence across all platforms dramatically increases how often you are mentioned, cited, or referenced in the answers to queries.

In ServiceFlow's case, most of the content Sarah and the team had produced lived on the website. This was working because ServiceFlow had exceptional organic SEO working in its favor.

"Crossing the threshold of 50 percent requires more distribution beyond just the ServiceFlow website," I explained. "This means we need to expand production across social media platforms."

"I feel like you're asking us to become an entirely different company," said Peter.

"Better to do it yourself as the market leader than be forced to do it as the competitor trying to catch up," I responded.

Social media was almost the essential and necessary precursor to AI. Without Social media, AI platforms would not be nearly as effective because the underlying training data would not exist.

Until Social media came along, buying happened in a straight line. You visited a website, scheduled a demo, talked to a sales rep, and decided to make a purchase.

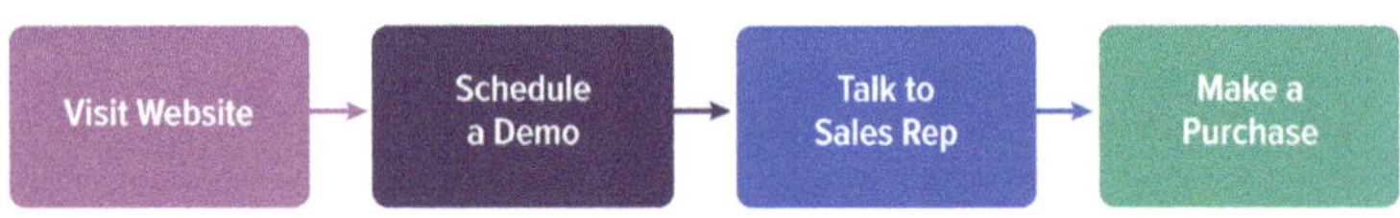

With social media, a lot of actions have become untrackable. You could have conversations, consume content, follow influencers, and join communities that directly impacted your buying decisions without ever talking to the company you eventually ended up buying from.

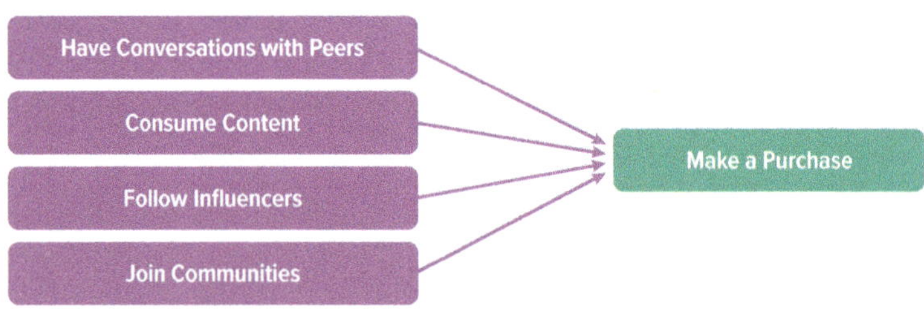

This "content"—whether in the form of videos on YouTube, threads on Reddit, answers on Quora, reviews on Capterra, posts on X, reels on Instagram, or transcripts from podcasts—dramatically increases the underlying training data set for AI platforms to build their answers on.

A company could have all the content in the world on its website, but a lack of presence on social media is like shutting off half the training data that AI platforms use to determine what to mention, cite, and reference in their answers to queries.

"We need a system to scale across platforms," I explained to Peter and Sarah. "That's the only way this works."

"Good, because I don't see how we have the time, people, or resources to do this," said Sarah.

"The trick is to create a content amplification model," I said in response.

"What does that mean?" asked Peter.

"We need an anchor content property."

BUILDING A CONTENT AMPLIFICATION MODEL

In an AI world, omnipresence across all platforms is critical. The more present you are, the more likely you are to be used in the training data and responses for all types of queries. Social media content expands the role of AI from just our best sales rep to the go-to expert that a prospect trusts across all stages of the buyer journey.

Why? Because with content for the ultra long-tail plus content to establish Iconic Positioning, an exceptional amount of training data is available to AI platforms to give the best possible answer for each query.

First, train AI like a Sales Rep. Then, train AI like an expert.

Train AI as a Sales Rep ➡️ **Train AI as an Expert**

To do this, distribution and scale are the key. The problem is that most companies do not have the resources to scale across all platforms. It's a gargantuan task to post on LinkedIn, Facebook, Instagram, X, YouTube, Reddit, podcasts, Spotify, Substack, and more, every single day.

You probably know media brands and personalities who do this and wonder how they keep up their publishing schedule. The difference is that those media brands and personalities are content-first companies. ESPN's entire business is to publish sports content and distribute it across all social platforms so you can watch games on their channels. Andrew Huberman's entire business is to publish health-related content and distribute it across all social platforms so you listen to his podcast so he can grow his audience and charge more for sponsorships or promote products he's involved with.

How is a company not in the media business supposed to keep up a publishing schedule like this? The short answer is you can't because you're in a different business.

But you can emulate it and come close. The way you do this is with a content amplification model. The model was first popularized by Gary Vaynerchuk back in 2018, who was omnipresent across all social platforms before most brands came close to figuring out how to do it. Now you have all kinds of influencers and thought leaders copying the same model.

"A content amplification model involves investing in an anchor content property," I explained to Peter and Sarah. "The anchor content property is a long-form piece of content published on a regular schedule, and it becomes the first domino in distributing content across all platforms."

Peter and Sarah were listening intently. "What would that look like for us?"

"That's up to us to decide," I answered. "It can be a podcast, a YouTube channel, a webinar series, a live cast, a conference, an online summit, or anything else."

Here's how it works:

1. You build an extensive roadmap of content (which we had already done for ServiceFlow)
2. You produce a long-form, anchor piece of content (podcast, video, etc.) that tries to address as many of the roadmap items
3. You promote the long-form, anchor content to your core audience
4. You then splice that long-form content into hundreds of smaller assets and distribute across all social platforms and profiles
5. You promote all the smaller, micro content across all platforms

This process simplifies and reduces the amount of work required to be omnipresent, while also building all the training data required to train AI platforms. It also removes the need for a massive team to do the work. You can do it with an agency or a couple of core team members.

This process is the main reason why the next decade will see all kinds of companies invest in major content platforms. You are going to see massive YouTube channels, podcasts, and Netflix specials being created by companies and brands. We've already seen it in the sports world with shows like *Drive To Survive* dramatically increasing F1 viewership through long-form content, along with all the short-form social content that goes with it.

With the results ServiceFlow was already seeing, Peter didn't need much more convincing to buy into the process. The company was growing, and he already had the board's buy-in.

"What's the best way for us to do this?" he asked.

"We need an anchor content property focused on our buyer."

CREATING ANCHOR CONTENT FOCUSED ON THE BUYER

For ServiceFlow, the ultimate decision-maker was always the business owner of a field service business. These people were small business entrepreneurs. They funded their entire business with their own money, time, and effort.

"My suggestion is we focus on these entrepreneurs," I said. "We should create content that helps them navigate all the challenges that come with running a field service business. Things no one else would truly understand."

"We've always talked about doing something like this," said Peter. "We just never got around to it."

Sarah, Peter, and I worked together to create a vision for a video podcast as the core piece of anchor content called the *Field Service Champions* podcast. Each episode:

- Would feature the owner of a field service business, breaking down their approach to operating and scaling their organization
- Covered one or many of the topics outlined in our content roadmap of over 16,000 items to build the underlying training data set to train AI like an expert in this market that views ServiceFlow as an authority in the space
- Brought up the topic of field service management software in the conversation organically, and the business owners got to naturally answer how they approached that topic
- Featured ServiceFlow sponsorship promos at the beginning, middle, and end of the episodes

To start, the episodes featured business owners from ServiceFlow's existing client base. It was the easiest place to start, given how many leading companies used ServiceFlow.

Each podcast:

- Was published on every podcast platform
- Had a corresponding transcript published on the ServiceFlow website
- Had a detailed blog post on the ServiceFlow website

Sarah and her team created a basic playbook to promote each episode:

- Email blast their subscriber and customer base about each episode
- Include the episode in their monthly newsletter
- Post each episode on ServiceFlow's social profiles
- Key leaders, sales reps, and executives share the episodes on their LinkedIn
- Episode guests and their companies promote the episode through their own LinkedIn, newsletter, and email lists

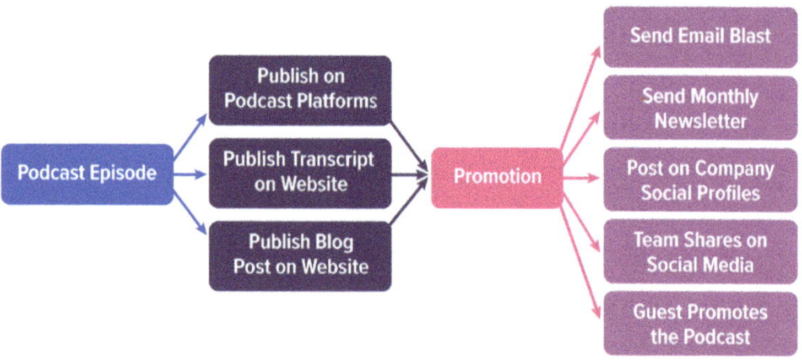

With just this simple playbook, ServiceFlow started getting over five hundred downloads per episode just a few months in. With each episode, the audience was growing.

In the market, there wasn't anyone really interviewing owners of field service management companies at the level of depth that ServiceFlow was on the *Field Service Champions* podcast. It was one of those markets that was ignored on the content front because the businesses were generally smaller in nature.

These business owners were starved for great content, and ServiceFlow was meeting that need with the *Field Service Champions* podcast.

"This is the right start, but we need to now scale distribution," I said to Sarah. "It's time to expand to all social platforms."

BECOMING CITATION-WORTHY WITH SOCIAL DISTRIBUTION

So far, producing the podcast had been fairly simple. Sarah and her team would find a guest, record the interview, edit the episode, publish the podcast, and promote the content through a standard playbook.

Now, we had to build the process to expand distribution to other social platforms. Here's how the process worked.

Each episode could be turned into over fifty pieces of content:

- Ten to fifteen short-form videos for YouTube Shorts, Instagram Reels, and TikTok
- Twenty to thirty text-only posts for LinkedIn and X
- Fifteen to twenty image plus text posts for LinkedIn, Instagram, and X

"I can see how this process will help us grow the podcast to over ten thousand downloads," said Sarah.

"That may happen, but let's not count on it," I said, tempering expectations. "Podcasts growing to that level rarely happen."

Sarah looked confused, "Then what's the point of taking on all this work?"

"We have built a repeatable process to rip through the 16,000 items we identified in our content roadmap to train the AI platforms," I explained. "That list will only grow as time goes on. We now have a process to run through it."

With each episode, ServiceFlow was building a massive repository of informational and educational content to answer all kinds of questions its ICP had about its pain points. Not only that, but each episode:

- Had a field service business owner discussing their approach in detail
- Showcased how other businesses could do the same, regardless of what type of field service business they were, with extreme detail and expertise
- Had video content to go with it, with long-form text explanations

This trifecta of content, expertise, and distribution gave ServiceFlow a massive advantage over its competitors in the market. No one else was investing in its Iconic Positioning in the marketplace.

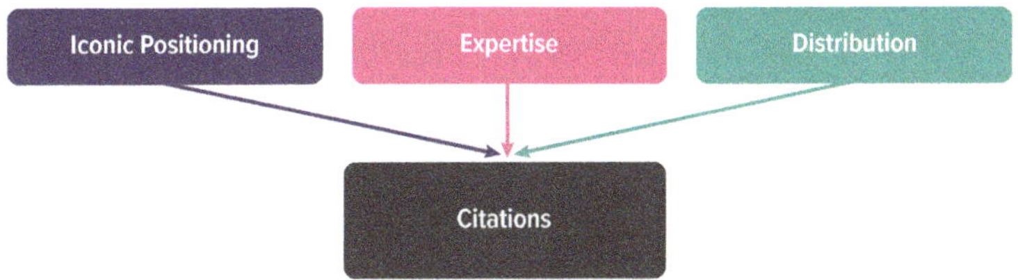

Again, AI platforms are looking for signals on how to answer one critical question: What is the best possible answer to this query, and *who* has the best possible answer to this question?

This playbook changed how AI platforms perceived ServiceFlow. Suddenly, ServiceFlow wasn't just a company creating content that only promoted its products.

ServiceFlow was now the go-to expert in its market for AI platforms.

This shift started to drive more mentions, citations, and references across the board for ServiceFlow. Just a few months in, the visibility metrics looked like this:

TYPE OF QUERY	VISIBILITY START (%)	VISIBILITY WITHOUT SOCIAL (%)	VISIBILITY WITH SOCIAL (%)
Navigational	72%	78%	83%
Informational	12%	17%	29%
Transactional	36%	39%	55%
Generative	5%	9%	12%

This was a colossal jump from before. With it, ServiceFlow was seeing a 25 percent increase in MQLs and Opportunities in its pipeline. This wasn't a coincidence.

"I can't believe it," said Peter. "Our podcast audience is still hovering around seven hundred downloads an episode, but we're showing up for so many more queries."

"That's because downloads and visibility are not directly correlated," I explained. "What is correlated is the expertise in the content and the engagement on social for that content."

"Our engagement on social posts has been really high," said Sarah. "We're getting thousands of views on each short video on social platforms and our posts on LinkedIn."

This was a key insight. Social engagement—impressions, views, likes, comments, shares, reposts, saves—is a critical signal for AI platforms to identify who has expertise. If you're an expert, then people should interact with you, right?

"This is why we now need to turn our attention to growing our audience."

YOUR TURN

3. Citation-Worthy Content

Identify one Anchor Content Property you will heavily invest in as a way to signal your expertise.

Follow these prompts to build an initial list:

- What content mediums are most popular with your ICP (video, audio, books, etc.)?
- What type of content property is most aligned with your business?
- What type of content is the best way to showcase your expertise?
- Which content can you repeatedly produce on a schedule and stay consistent?

Get the full workbook at: www.howtosaas.com/blueprint.

CHAPTER 4

GROWING A FOLLOWING WITH AUTHENTIC EXPERTISE

1. Prequalification	2. Iconic Positioning	3. Citation-Worthy Content	4. Authenticity and Originality
Create a list of fifteen to twenty-five long-tail self-education queries to prequalify your ICP.	*Create a list of five to ten adjacent problem areas your ICP is facing beyond the scope of your solution.*	*Identify one Anchor Content Property you will heavily invest into as a way to signal your expertise.*	*Build one proprietary process, framework, or approach to help your ICP navigate their core pain points.*

Download at howtosaas.com/blueprint

"I have a serious question," said Sarah. "This roadmap is so extensive. Why not just use AI to write the content for us? We could move so much faster."

It was a reasonable question. Sarah also wasn't alone in thinking this way.

Ever since ChatGPT emerged, the world has been flooded with AI-generated content. As time goes on, it will only get worse. We are already at a point where it is difficult to distinguish between AI-generated and human-generated content.

This is the negative long-term externality of AI—extreme content commoditization, and more noise than ever before. In a world with so much noise and ubiquitous content, the real currency is creativity and authenticity.

"What do you think is the number one reason the podcast has been growing?" I asked Sarah, answering her question with a question.

"Because we're creating content for our audience in a way that no one else is," Sarah responded.

"That's partially correct," I said. "The number one reason is actually that Peter is doing the interviews."

I wasn't trying to give Peter undue credit. Sarah was right that the strategy and roadmap we had laid out were a big reason that the podcast was growing. However, the big differentiator was that Peter was the host and interviewer on all the episodes.

Before Peter had started ServiceFlow, he had himself built, scaled, and exited an eight-figure landscaping business. That's where he got the idea for ServiceFlow in the first place. He was the customer. Peter's experience made every conversation significantly more valuable. He was able to talk about strategy, operations, service design, resourcing, marketing, sales, people, hiring, and much more with every guest in a way not many people could.

This one distinction is an asset that no other brand or company in the space had as an asset.

When companies do not have someone like Peter, they resort to research and data as a substitute for true expertise. For example, a competitor could publish an asset like "Benchmarking Operating Expenses for Field Service Companies" as a proxy for the expertise of someone like Peter, who can give a more direct recommendation. Another proxy could be to bring in outside expertise to partner with your brand since you don't have that expertise in-house. For example, Shopify could use successful e-commerce entrepreneurs to educate prospects on how to build a great online store and business.

These types of proxies are still valuable and a good way to distinguish yourself as a company if you don't have someone like Peter. They also scale because it doesn't always require the founder. The best mix is actually being able to do both. Having a founder or CEO who is an expert and out there is a huge asset. At the same time, using other proxies can help you scale faster.

"Peter's experience gives something to the podcast that is impossible to replace," I explained.

"What's that?" asked Sarah.

"Credibility."

"Most content is second-party content," I continued. "It is downstream from other content that already exists."

The simplest example of this is sports content. A tennis match or basketball game happens, which is the primary content. The secondary content is the hundreds of clips and plays published and distributed across thousands of user accounts and notable profiles. The tertiary content is the commentary shows and podcasts about those same matches, which are then spliced into further pieces of micro-content distributed across thousands of profiles.

The same happens with reality shows, movies, documentaries, concerts, speaking events, songs, podcasts, and books. The aftermarket of content is extensive. There are so many providers of this "secondary and tertiary content" that it's getting harder for users to distinguish between them. It's just more noise. No one really remembers where they saw the secondary or tertiary content.

The real value is in being the primary source of the content. People remember the NBA, *Love Is Blind*, *Drive To Survive,* and The Eras Tour.

What's more is that AI regurgitates what is already out there. After all, all its outputs are present in the training data. How can it create something entirely new and groundbreaking if it was never in its training data set?

This is the value of true expertise. Originality. In a world of commoditized, AI-generated content, true expertise is an anomaly. It's like finding a black swan. AI values this originality as well because it helps answer queries that previously could not be answered.

"What Peter brings to the podcast with his expertise is first-party content," I continued. "He's bringing authentic, original expertise to the audience. If we leverage AI to create that content for us, we will lose that secret sauce."

Sarah looked like a lightbulb had just turned on above her head, "Authentic expertise trumps volume, then."

"I couldn't have said it better myself," I confirmed. "We need to lean more into Peter's expertise for all our customers, and then we need to scale it."

One challenge with the *Field Service Champions* podcast was that Peter was the interviewer, not the interviewee. Each episode highlighted the guest much more, for obvious reasons, as Peter asked questions to extract insights. Peter would do his best to interject and add anecdotes and tidbits along the way, but the episode was always still about the guest.

With this approach, most episodes became a way to showcase guests' expertise, not Peter's and ServiceFlow's. There were benefits to this, of course, but the downside was that Peter and ServiceFlow weren't showcasing all their original ideas.

"We need to add a layer that focuses on Peter's expertise," I said to Sarah and Peter.

"What's the best way to do that?" asked Peter.

"We need you to create more content from scratch."

CREATING ORIGINAL CONTENT

"I feel like we are already doing that," said Peter.

"We are," I reassured him. "But we need to create a system that is original to ServiceFlow."

"What do you mean?" Peter asked.

"You have all this expertise from building your last business," I explained. "You need to turn that into a framework that can be used by all other business owners. Something that can be applied to all field service companies."

This was a revelation to Peter. All these years, he had just been helping all kinds of field service companies on his own instincts. Within a thirty-minute conversation, he'd know exactly what those companies needed to address and solve to scale faster because he had lived it before. Each business owner and company he met had its own nuances, but they were also very much alike. Over time, he got really good at quickly diagnosing problems and taking the right actions to resolve them.

This skill set was what he brought to sales calls during the first couple of years at ServiceFlow when he was the main closer to deals. It earned a ton of trust from clients and got them to sign up even when ServiceFlow was not nearly as big as the larger incumbents in the space.

"That trust and credibility you built with your expertise with customers early on," I continued, "we need to scale that with content."

I asked Peter to walk Sarah and me through how to scale a field service business. Over the next two hours, Peter put on a masterclass for us in ServiceFlow's conference room. He talked about all kinds of concepts that many business coaches would charge $10,000 for a two-day event.

Peter walked us through:

- How to start a new field service company
- How different types of field service companies (electricians, plumbers, landscapers, etc.) all deal with different problems
- The different strategies to scale each type of field service company
- The different stages of field service companies and the challenges at each stage
- The right operational model at each stage of a field service company
- How to scale a field service company to different cities and regions
- People issues that each field service company deals with at each stage
- How to structure a field service organization to scale

Sarah was blown away. She had always respected Peter's leadership as the CEO but she had never seen the depth of his expertise in this way before. When it came to content and marketing, he just left things to her.

"None of our content is this good, Peter," she said finally. "We need to put you everywhere."

"Peter, that was incredible," I said in agreement. "We need to take all this and organize it into a proprietary framework that is synonymous with you and ServiceFlow."

Running a playbook like this isn't possible for every company because not every company has someone like Peter. In a world with AI, people like Peter are a huge asset to companies. The best founders help position their companies in the marketplace. If they are true experts that the market wants to follow, it creates a much bigger moat around the business.

Generally, people like to follow people, not brands. No one really follows Virgin, but people follow Richard Branson. People don't follow movie studios, they follow movie stars. People may be fans of sports teams, but they follow players a lot more. There's a reason people started watching MLS after Messi went to Inter Miami. It's the same reason why people follow Tobi Lutke more than Shopify.

The same is true for companies. In a world with AI, companies need personalities to plant their flag in their domain of expertise. You have exceptions, of course, especially with really large companies. In general, however, having a person lead the charge in the market can help companies grow a lot faster.

Sarah and I worked closely with Peter to pull together and distill his expertise into a system that could be mapped to a wide range of field service companies.

We called it *The Field Service Growth Playbook*. This wasn't a white paper that companies publish on their resources page. It was a dissertation with true expertise on how to truly build a field service company from the ground up.

The playbook also included variations for each vertical that ServiceFlow helped. There was a step-by-step framework for plumbers, electricians, contractors, landscapers, roofers, painters, and more.

This wasn't just about the 16,000 items we had previously identified for our roadmap. Peter's expertise had opened up an entirely new domain of content for ServiceFlow.

As we made progress, it became clear that this wasn't just something that should live behind a landing page on the ServiceFlow website. Peter had just written a book that every field service business owner needed to read.

Over the next 6 months, we found a publisher to work with us to publish the book. Sarah and her team took the lead on the book launch and promotion. The big push was to ServiceFlow's existing customers, prospects, and email subscribers. Peter also actively promoted the book through the podcast on every episode.

"This isn't just about AI," I said to Peter. "This book is going to change how the entire market perceives you."

Peter's book became an Amazon bestseller in the first week, which in itself was a big accomplishment. What was bigger was all the other benefits that came with it.

Peter started speaking at one or two events and podcasts every single month, some virtual, some in person. From this alone, ServiceFlow saw an increase in pipeline. At each event, ServiceFlow would give away Peter's books for free.

Slowly, more and more people were reading the book. With the podcast and now the book, small business owners of field service companies started to view Peter as a thought leader in their space.

Sarah and her team leaned into this. All the content from the book served as a source material for all other content that ServiceFlow was producing across all channels. Blog posts, videos, social media posts, and reels all featured ServiceFlow actively promoting Peter's frameworks, often with Peter's face as the thought leader discussing the concepts.

Not only did this grow Peter and ServiceFlow's audience across the board, but it also created a secondary market of content. All kinds of customers were reviewing the book, sharing it on their social media profiles, discussing it on podcasts, and even creating videos about the book's takeaways. This user-generated content significantly increased ServiceFlow's social footprint.

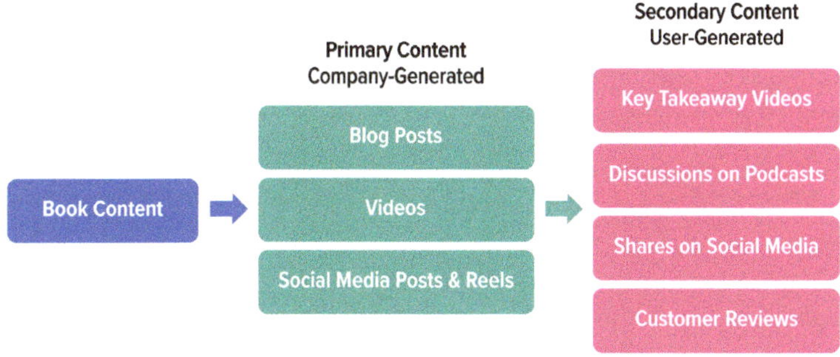

The AI platforms noticed as well. ServiceFlow now had:

- An Amazon book
- Amazon reviews
- Podcasts interviewing Peter on his book
- Conference videos of Peter speaking
- Users posting and recommending Peter's book on all platforms

On top of this, the AI platforms had a whole bunch of new training data, built on true expertise, for multiple queries related to growing field service companies. It had a go-to expert it could rely on for queries like:

- What's the fastest way to scale a landscaping company to other cities?
- What is the right structure for the leadership team of my $10 million roofing business that operates in five cities across Texas?
- How do I improve retention rates for my plumbing business?

That's when everything took off. Visibility skyrocketed across AI platforms:

TYPE OF QUERY	VISIBILITY START (%)	VISIBILITY NOW (%)
Navigational	72%	89%
Informational	12%	45%
Transactional	36%	68%
Generative	5%	17%

This change impacted all metrics across the board for ServiceFlow:

- Podcast listenership went up 200 percent
- Pipeline went up 24 percent
- Opportunity to Close Rates increased by 30 percent

Prospects were showing up to sales calls either with Peter's book in hand, having listened to him on the podcast, or having heard him speak. The visibility on AI platforms was almost secondary.

Peter and ServiceFlow's position in the market had become iconic.

"I guess our work here is done?" said Peter half jokingly.

"Not even close," I responded.

"What's left?" he asked.

"We haven't even gotten to leveraging product and sales."

YOUR TURN

4. Authenticity and Originality

Build one proprietary process, framework, or approach to help your ICP navigate their core pain points.

Follow these prompts to build an initial list:

- What is your biggest source of credibility in this market?
- What is something your founder or business is uniquely positioned to speak on?
- What is an earned secret that no one else in the market would easily have access to?

Get the full workbook at: www.howtosaas.com/blueprint.

CHAPTER 5

LEVERAGING PRODUCT FOR MULTI-VARIATE PROBLEMS

1. Prequalification	2. Iconic Positioning	3. Citation-Worthy Content	4. Authenticity and Originality
Create a list of fifteen to twenty-five long-tail self-education queries to prequalify your ICP.	*Create a list of five to ten adjacent problem areas your ICP is facing beyond the scope of your solution.*	*Identify one Anchor Content Property you will heavily invest into as a way to signal your expertise.*	*Build one proprietary process, framework, or approach to help your ICP navigate their core pain points.*
5. Product Levers			
Identify three to five product tools that can help your ICP solve their problems without necessarily buying your full solution.			

Download at howtosaas.com/blueprint

"There's one anomaly in our visibility numbers," I said. "Did you notice that the Generative queries are not going up at the same rate?"

"I did notice that," said Peter. "What does that mean?"

TYPE OF QUERY	VISIBILITY START (%)	VISIBILITY NOW (%)
Navigational	72%	89%
Informational	12%	45%
Transactional	36%	68%
Generative	5%	17%

"It means that when people use AI to create something new," I explained, "we are not nearly as visible as we should be."

The first three types of queries are still information based. Customers make queries, and the platform answers them. Generative queries are different in nature. They ask AI platforms to create something new.

Here are some examples:

- Create a marketing plan to ramp up leads for my landscaping company.
- I need a loan for my roofing business. What kind of terms should I be looking for? Model out the interest versus principal payments.
- Help me build a business case for investing in additional machinery for my construction company.
- Help me design the right compensation plan for the COO of a plumbing company.
- Here is the P&L for my HVAC business. What adjustments should I make to increase my EBITDA?

"Aren't these types of queries similar to the queries we've been creating content for?" asked Sarah.

"Yes, but with one important difference," I answered. "These queries are multi-variate problems with multi-variate solutions."

LEVERAGING PRODUCT FOR GENERATIVE QUERIES

Queries with multivariate problems present a unique challenge. You cannot solve them with a simple article or piece of content. Let's use the example of a query looking for loan terms for the roofing business. All these factors come into play:

- How big is the loan?
- How big is the business in terms of revenue?
- How profitable is the business?
- How much debt does the business currently have?
- What are the financial projections for the next 12–24 months?
- How much personal debt does the business owner have?
- Does the owner have enough personal cash to cover the loan if needed?

There are several more questions to ask to give a proper answer to that initial query. Trying to solve this problem with an article is a fool's errand. There are simply too many variables.

Many companies try to circumvent these issues by writing really long guides. For example, to answer the query on compensation plans for COOs, they'll write a one-hundred-page document with compensation plans segmented by company type, size, city, and much more.

The problem is that no one reads this content. Even if anyone does, fewer people will read it going forward.

It's much easier to just ask an AI platform for your specific situation. For example, "I run a $10 million construction company and am looking for a COO. We're bootstrapped and don't have external investors. I'd like to grant the employee equity in the form of options. We're based in Norfolk, Virginia. Give me a compensation plan to hire an A-player."

The question can be answered in seconds instead of downloading a one-hundred-page guide behind a landing page.

"These are the queries we need to enable," I explained to Peter.

"If a guide isn't the way to do this, then how do we do it?" he asked.

"We need help from your product team," I answered.

One of the things companies get wrong on the product side is that they think the product's role starts at the point where the user actually uses their solution. This has historically been very wrong. The reason is that users interact with your business well before they ever enter your actual product. Limiting those interactions to only marketing and sales material is a mistake.

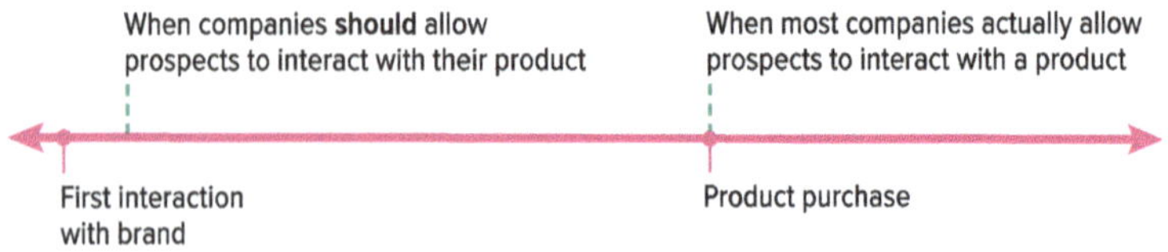

Your end solution may be the most comprehensive version of what you are selling, but before customers experience that solution, there are several opportunities for them to interact with a "product" from you beyond your core solution.

HubSpot popularized this idea with their website grader tool in the early 2010s. Shopify has a logo maker. Banks have mortgage calculators. Canva has pre-made templates. In fact, if you analyze the traffic data for companies like Canva, their "Templates" pages get some of the most traffic for a reason.

In a world with AI, this is even more important. When presented with Generative queries, AI platforms need tools to address multivariate problems and provide productive answers. Without these tools, AI is scouring the internet and training itself on long-form articles, making assumptions, and giving the best possible estimate.

For example, if your mortgage is up for renewal and you ask AI to give you options, it can go to every bank's website, go through its mortgage calculators, and give you real estimates of what you should expect. In this scenario, the AI platform is almost playing the role of a mortgage broker for you. It doesn't have the relationships at the banks to get you a favorable rate, but it can certainly give you an accurate, timely estimate of what you expect.

These kinds of queries are essential to have "content" for. They're not content in a traditional sense. They require the product team. The long-term value of developing these items in an AI world is far more interactions with customers and far more visibility for Generative queries.

"What would these queries even look like?" Peter asked.

"We need to take the expertise we put into *The Field Service Growth Playbook* and combine it with product tools," I answered.

UNDERSTANDING THE DEPTH AND BREADTH OF GENERATIVE QUERIES

The goal was to create a path to interactions with buyers before they had used the product to support them with problems they were facing in their business. I worked with Peter and Sarah to expand on the content inside *The Field Service Growth Playbook* into buckets of Generative queries.

Here's what we came up with (note: this is not the full exhaustive list):

Quotes and Invoices

- Create a custom quote for a client with the following specifications.
- Turn this text message from the customer into a formal estimate and send it.
- Create an invoice for a customer based on this contract.

Scheduling and Dispatch

- Create a custom route for my techs for these addresses to minimize drive time.
- Assign techs to jobs based on job type and location.
- Schedule this job next week at the earliest time when a qualified tech is available.

Customer Intake & Job Creation

- Take this email thread and create a job with the right customer info, scope, and notes.
- Create a customer intake form with the following questions.
- Create an appointment booking and scheduler for prospective clients.

Payments & Collections

- Send the invoice with a payment form and checkout.
- Tell me which of my invoices are overdue.
- Reconcile yesterday's payments with QuickBooks.

Purchasing, Materials, POs

- Create a purchase order for materials for next week's jobs and tomorrow's job, and send them to the supplier.
- Compare Home Depot versus supplier pricing for this materials list and pick the cheapest delivered option.
- Analyze current materials stock from inventory and flag shortages.

Job Documentation & Closeout

- Generate a completion report with before/after photos and send them to the customer.
- Create a warranty certificate for this job.
- Write the job notes professionally from these technician bullet points.

HR & Payroll

- Turn today's job timeline into timesheets for each tech.
- Flag any job where labor hours exceeded estimates by 25 percent.
- Summarize weekly productivity: jobs per day, revenue per hour, callbacks.

Custom Solutions

- Set up my service catalog for roofing: repairs, replacements, inspections—with suggested prices.
- Create job templates, checklists, and invoice templates for my business.
- Give me a basic way to track my pipeline for leads, appointments, quotes, closed won, and invoices.

Types of Generative Queries	Outcome
Quotes and Invoices	• Create a custom quote for a client with the following specifications • Turn this text message from the customer into a formal estimate and send it • Create an invoice for a customer based on this contract
Scheduling and Dispatch	• Create a custom route for my techs for these addresses to minimize drive time • Assign techs to jobs based on job type and location • Schedule this job next week at the earliest time when a qualified tech is available
Customer Intake and Job Creation	• Take this email thread and create a job with the right customer info, scope, and notes • Create a customer intake form with the following questions • Create an appointment booking and scheduler for prospective clients
Payments and Collections	• Send the invoice with a payment form and checkout • Tell me which of my invoices are overdue • Reconcile yesterday's payments with QuickBooks
Purchasing, Materials, POs	• Create a purchase order for materials for next week's jobs/tomorrow's jobs and send them to the supplier • Compare Home Depot versus supplier pricing for this materials list and pick the cheapest delivered option • Analyze current materials stock from inventory and flag shortages
Job Documentation and Closeout	• Generate a completion report with before/after photos and send them to the customer • Create a warranty certificate for this job • Write the job notes professionally from these technician bullet points
HR and Payroll	• Turn today's job timeline into timesheets for each tech • Flag any job where labor hours exceeded estimates by 25 percent • Summarize weekly productivity: jobs per day, revenue per hour, callbacks
Custom Solutions	• Set up my service catalog for roofing: repairs, replacements, inspections—with suggested prices • Create job template, checklists, and invoice templates for my business • Give me a basic way to track my pipeline for leads, appointments, quotes, closed won, and invoices

"What do you notice about this list?" I asked Peter.

"They're completely different from the list of queries we created earlier," he answered.

"Exactly," I responded.

We reviewed the exhaustive list of queries and reexamined ServiceFlow's visibility metrics. Here is what we found:

TYPE OF QUERY	VISIBILITY START (%)	VISIBILITY NOW (%)
Navigational	72%	89%
Informational	12%	45%
Transactional	36%	68%
Generative	5%	12%

"Notice how our visibility for Generative queries actually decreased," I said, pointing to the data. "It's because we expanded the list to include multi-variate queries, and we simply do not have the right tools to address those queries."

Peter understood the problem. He had Aleem, his VP of Product, get plugged into the initiative.

Aleem listened and then finally said, "We're already swamped with getting through our roadmap."

This was expected. Product teams in general are resistant to having Marketing and Sales direct their efforts. Needless to say, this back and forth went on for some time.

"Aleem, this work will help us scale our users faster," insisted Peter. "We need to de-prioritize nonessential items to make room for this work."

"The key thing to wrap your head around is that this work *is* product work," I said to Aleem. "This is one of the most forgotten roles of product."

"What role is that?" asked Aleem, buying into the idea.

"To help acquire new customers," I explained.

BUILDING TOOLS FOR GENERATIVE QUERIES

"Do you notice a common theme on the list of Generative queries we built?" I asked Aleem.

"A lot of them involved capabilities already inside our product," he answered correctly.

"Yes," I confirmed. "The only difference is that the people who will make those queries are not ServiceFlow customers."

These kinds of queries—like creating an invoice, quote, or purchase order—were core capabilities of ServiceFlow. If a prospect didn't have ServiceFlow, they still needed to solve that problem. Most software prospects in almost all industries are in "Excel Hell," using spreadsheets or Google Docs to create solutions and manage everything. They often graduate to software when spreadsheets become too complex to address their specific pain point. For example, you can use a spreadsheet as a CRM or project management tool as a one-person business, but at some point, you need something like HubSpot and Trello to manage everything.

In a world with AI, an "intermediate" solution is created. You don't need QuickBooks right away because you can create an invoice without the grunt work of doing it manually on Google Docs by simply asking ChatGPT to create it for you. This allows you to find some automation, which reduces some of the headache, and is still cheaper than buying the full software solution.

This intermediate step is the opportunity in the buyer journey, where Product can drive visibility across all AI platforms.

In recent years, Satya Nadella, Sam Altman, Jensen Huang, and several other technology leaders have shaken up the world of software by claiming that agents will eventually replace all software. No one really fully understood what that actually means or what it will look like. But as AI technologies have evolved, companies across the board have been investing in making their platforms AI-first or AI-enabled. Every website you go to has "AI-Powered" somewhere in its main heading or subtext, above the fold.

On the product side, there is a clearer understanding of what this is supposed to look like. For example, having AI capabilities inside Salesforce allows you to enrich data, get concise summaries of sales calls, and predict which deals to focus on based on the likelihood of closing. Leveraging AI capabilities inside Shopify lets you dynamically update product images, craft email campaigns, and convert live chat into checkouts. This kind of innovation—that combines data capabilities, product, and AI—is something virtually all companies are working on.

"We're doing a lot of the product work already," confirmed Peter. "I've already got the team working on AI capabilities to help our customers speed up areas like quoting, payments, and workforce management."

"What not enough companies are not working on yet is leveraging data, product, and AI to build tools that service the buyer journey at earlier stages of the funnel," I explained to Peter. "This is the real opportunity in front of us."

"We need to create a series of tools that address Generative queries at this intermediate step," I continued. "The good news is that a lot of these Generative queries can be grouped together and addressed by a handful of tools."

On our list of Generative queries, here were the big areas of focus:

- Quoting
- Invoicing
- Customer Intake
- Sales
- Scheduling
- Dispatch
- Payments

"We need lightweight solutions that address all of these," I explained.

I proceeded to work with Aleem to create a list of seven tools that would help us address a big chunk of the Generative queries. Here are the tools we came up with:

1. Invoice and Estimate Engine
2. Calendar Availability and Appointment Booking
3. Customer Intake Forms
4. Routing and ETA Mapper
5. Materials Cost Comparison Calculator
6. Timesheets and Job Costing
7. Job Documentation Reports

None of these tools was a full solution by any means. They were lightweight tools that allowed prospects and AI platforms to address queries that were previously unaddressed. There was a big difference between what the tools would do and what they wouldn't do.

TOOL	CAPABILITIES	NOT INCLUDED
Invoice and Estimates	Create PDFs of invoices based on text messages, images, and basic descriptions	Not connected to QuickBooks or other invoicing system
Appointment booking	Calendar availability and bookings	Not connected to CRM or automations
Customer Intake	Forms with standardized questions	Not connected to project management
Routing and ETA Mapper	Build daily routes with Google Maps	Not connected to open projects and workforce
Materials and Cost Comparison Calculator	Compare supplier pricing across multiple vendors	Not able to send purchase orders
Timesheets and Job Costing	Templates to estimate total costs to finish jobs	Not connected to payroll platforms
Job Documentation	Create job completion reports with before and after photos	Not connected to CRM or project management

With these limitations, Aleem and the Product team were able to design and ship these tools without extensive development cycles. Because a lot of the capabilities were already in the ServiceFlow platform, building the tools was much faster than expected.

I also had Aleem and the Product team prioritize applications for the AI platforms themselves. Companies like Canva were already doing this. For example, you can create designs inside ChatGPT without ever going to Canva's website and platform. We wanted

ServiceFlow to be able to provide the same. Each of the above tools had an application inside ChatGPT, Gemini, and other AI tools. With this, the user never had to leave the AI platforms.

AI platforms now also had tools they could query for multivariate problems. Just a few months after the tools went live, the visibility for Generative queries started to jump up:

TYPE OF QUERY	VISIBILITY START (%)	VISIBILITY NOW (%)
Navigational	72%	89%
Informational	12%	45%
Transactional	36%	68%
Generative	5%	35%

The AI platforms not only saw Peter and ServiceFlow as experts with iconic positioning now. They were being seen as providers of productized expertise. We had leveraged Peter's expertise and embedded it into free tools available to the market at large to build a successful field service business.

"You have to keep working on this," I explained to Aleem and Peter. "There should be a certain percentage of your product resources constantly developing tools like this so that there are more and more Generative queries being addressed."

Aleem was fully bought-in now that he could see the impact on the business with just a few of the basic tools he had created with his team. These tools had helped ServiceFlow grow faster than a lot of other major product initiatives he had worked on with his team over the years.

"We now need to shift our attention to distribution again," I said to Peter. "As the product team creates more tools, the AI platforms will continue to use those tools to address queries. We now need to find a way to amplify our reach beyond what will happen organically."

"I thought we had addressed distribution already with the content work we did?" asked Peter.

"We've done a lot of the organic work," I explained. "It's now time to focus on paid distribution."

YOUR TURN

5. Product Levers

Identify three to five product tools that can help your ICP solve their problems without necessarily buying your full solution.

Follow these prompts to build an initial list:

- What are some multivariate problems that your ICP is trying to solve for?
- What is a lightweight version of your full solution / modules that can be used to address Generative queries?
- What kinds of integrations can you build into existing AI platforms?

Get the full workbook at: www.howtosaas.com/blueprint.

CHAPTER 6

AMPLIFYING REACH WITH PAID DISTRIBUTION

1. Prequalification	2. Iconic Positioning	3. Citation-Worthy Content	4. Authenticity and Originality
Create a list of fifteen to twenty-five long-tail self-education queries to prequalify your ICP.	*Create a list of five to ten adjacent problem areas your ICP is facing beyond the scope of your solution.*	*Identify one Anchor Content Property you will heavily invest into as a way to signal your expertise.*	*Build one proprietary process, framework, or approach to help your ICP navigate their core pain points.*

5. Product Levers	6. Paid Distribution	
Identify three to five product tools that can help your ICP solve their problems without necessarily buying your full solution.	*Choose one to two paid media channels to invest into to amplify the reach, visibility, brand recall, and affinity of your content and solution.*	

Download at howtosaas.com/blueprint

"Declining paid media performance was one of the first things you both shared with me when we first met," I said to Peter and Sarah.

"It's funny you said that," replied Sarah. "When we first met, cost per click was up 47 percent year-over-year, click-through rates were down 23 percent, and our customer acquisition cost had increased by 62 percent."

"And now?" I asked.

"Performance has improved by quite a bit," continued Sarah. "CPC is still higher but only about 15 percent, CTR is down by only 7 percent. The problem is our paid media CAC is still up by 22 percent compared to previous years."

"I had asked Sarah to scale back our spending by about 50 percent when we first met," added Peter. "We haven't increased it since then because I wanted to see this process through with you."

The numbers Sarah shared were about what I had expected. By investing heavily in content for the long-tail of self-education, building authority, anchor content through the podcast, building a following with the book and speaking, and leveraging product to drive more inbound interactions, ServiceFlow had given itself a major boost across all channels.

One of the secondary benefits of all the work we had done so far was that ServiceFlow's brand and market presence had grown significantly. This meant that any time a customer was presented with options on any channel, platform, or medium, they had pre-built trust with ServiceFlow and Peter, which made it far more likely for them to interact, engage, and convert.

Every week, I hear from founders that they've tried investing in ads on different platforms without much success. Every company ends up trying certain plays—LinkedIn Ads, Meta Ads, YouTube pre-roll Ads. Inevitably, most of them fail. Why? Because those companies don't have any pre-built trust.

"Pre-built trust is a huge currency in a world with AI," I explained to Sarah and Peter. "And you have built a ton of that now with the work we've done."

"It totally feels like it, but I worry about investing aggressively again into paid media," shared Peter. "That spend could easily go into more profitable channels."

"With the Iconic Positioning you've established in the market, paid media will be one of your most profitable channels," I reassured him.

"How do you know it will work this time?" he asked.

"Because content and demand generation scale proportionately to brand."

THE CONNECTION BETWEEN BRAND AND PERFORMANCE MARKETING

"When we first met, Branded Search had declined by almost 30 percent," I reminded Sarah and Peter. "Where are those numbers now?"

"I haven't checked those numbers in a couple of weeks," said Sarah as she started to look up the metrics. She paused when the numbers finally came up on the screen, then finally said, "I don't believe it. Branded Search traffic is up by 47 percent from our previous highs."

"That can't be right," said Peter in disbelief.

"It is," confirmed Sarah.

This shouldn't have been a surprise to Peter and Sarah. All the work we had done so far had drastically increased Service-Flow'smarket presence and its positioning and visibility on AI platforms. As each of those grew, more and more people started searching for ServiceFlow directly.

"This bump is not accidental," I explained. "This is the same reason why all organic numbers are up and why paid media performance started rebounding. ServiceFlow has a lot of pre-built trust in the market."

Coming back to the twenty-five Sales Questions we covered, the customer is really trying to choose the option that gives them the highest odds of success. From the customer's perspective, pre-built trust short-circuits all those questions, helping them make the right decision.

Unaware	Awareness	Education	Consideration	Decision
1. What is the trigger event causing this pain?	6. What is the actual problem?	11. Where should they search for a solution?	16. What are the alternatives?	21. What is the ROI of this investment?
2. What are the symptoms/pain experienced?	7. How common/big is this problem?	12. Who would know how to solve this problem?	17. Which alternative is the right one for their solution?	22. What kinds of results have others experienced?
3. What is the mistaken belief about solving the pain?	8. What is the cost of not solving this problem?	13. How have others solved this problem?	18. What is the right amount of money needed to solve this problem?	23. Whose buy-in do they need?
4. How are they currently solving this problem?	9. What kind of inertia do they need to overcome?	14. What is the right way to solve this problem?	19. How long will it take to solve this problem?	24. What's the risk if this doesn't work out?
5. What kind of revelation do they need to have?	10. How much can their life be transformed if they solve this problem?	15. How much is solving this problem worth to them?	20. Which alternative has the highest odds of success?	25. Why should they get started now?

This process is happening in real time every time the customer is faced with the inertia of multiple options like when they:

- Watch a YouTube video or listen to a podcast on how to grow their landscaping business
- Do a Google search for the best Field Service Management software
- Ask ChatGPT or Gemini to compare the feature sets of the top five providers of Field Service Management software
- Build a business case for which solution to ultimately pick for their plumbing company

There's a reason why the saying goes, "No one ever got fired for choosing Salesforce." It's a cliche, but it is also very true. A lot of organizations even struggle with Salesforce, don't have the internal talent to manage its clunkiness, and often burn a lot more budget than they should on the system. But it's Salesforce, so it has to be the right CRM for every business, right? Of course not.

"Let's do one more," I asked Sarah. "Let's pull up Branded Search Volumes for all of our competitors."

Sarah obliged and put together a basic dashboard. To her and Peter's surprise, yet again, ServiceFlow's volumes were more than 50 percent higher than those of other options in the market. Historically, ServiceFlow was often third in search volume in this market. It had suddenly jumped in the last year as we ran through the playbook.

In a pre-internet, mobile, social, and AI world of advertising, one of the most powerful metrics used by companies was something called Brand Recall. It represents the customer's ability to remember a brand when thinking of a category. For example, if we say running shoes, people often think of Nike. If we say smartphones, you might say Apple or iPhone.

There is also Aided Recall, which is a customer's ability to identify brands from a list or prompt. For example, "Are you familiar with JPMorgan Chase?"

Brand Recall—aided or unaided—is still widely used across industries like consumer packaged goods and retail. It's also used by really big brands like Salesforce, DocuSign, or QuickBooks because the bigger you get, the more important it becomes. It's important to know whether people think of HubSpot or Salesforce first when asked about CRM software and how they are trending against that.

Brand Recall is closely tied to another concept: Brand Affinity, the deep emotional connection customers feel toward a particular brand. You could have high Brand Recall but low Brand Affinity because customers don't really like your brand. A great example of this could be your internet or mobile provider. You may think of their name, but you likely don't like their product or service.

Unfortunately, smaller companies don't think about Brand Recall and Brand Affinity. They don't do enough surveys with customers (or use the results to guide their Go-To-Market), they don't track Branded Search Volume and Direct Traffic as a core KPI, they don't use NPS scores or CSAT ratings to make improvements, they don't track social media mentions and sentiment, they don't go through user-generated content or customer reviews, they don't track content consumption metrics on all platforms, and they don't analyze their customer lifetime data.

Brand Affinity and Recall Data Points

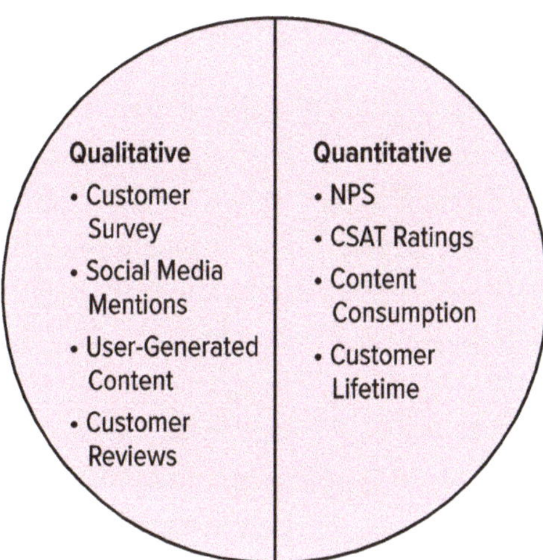

This is because smaller companies don't have enough resources to track and analyze all this data or run extensive voice-of-customer studies to conduct a deep dive into the value of their overall brand. Brand conversations inside companies often shrink to look and feel, the name, design, tag lines, and such. The real conversations about how customers perceive the brand don't happen often enough.

Yet, the brand exists in the marketplace. It's a living thing that is constantly evolving. The more you invest in it, the better your Brand Recall and Affinity. The better your Brand Recall and Affinity, the better your performance marketing.

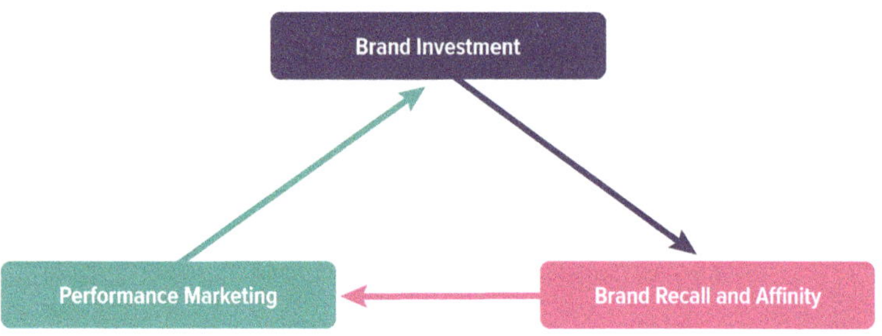

In most companies where "LinkedIn Ads didn't work" or "Google Ads became too expensive," the answer is often tied to a weak brand, weak positioning, and weak creative. In ServiceFlow's case, the issue was that they were operating in an ultracompetitive marketplace, competing with much larger incumbents. Building a stronger brand was the only way to make paid media performance work.

With the *Field Service Champions* podcast, *The Field Service Growth Playbook*, Peter speaking, and the product work to create tools to support buyers, ServiceFlow had been growing its Brand Recall and Affinity significantly.

"The Branded Volume metrics confirm what we need to do next," I said to Peter. "It's time we get much more aggressive with our paid media spend."

SCALING PAID MEDIA TO DRIVE DISTRIBUTION

"One of the reasons why both paid media and organic traffic had declined when we first met was simply because of real estate," I explained to Sarah and Peter.

"Because of AI Overviews at the top of Google Search results, you mean?" asked Sarah.

"Yes, partially," I answered. "Also because the real estate for visibility moved to AI platforms."

Real estate is a good way to visualize customer entry points. Historically, real estate would look like:

- The top three to four ads at the top of a Google Search query
- The next five to ten organic links below that query
- The rankings on listing sites that often ranked in both of those queries

If you were to take these three key pieces of real estate, you could tie overall paid and organic performance to how often you showed up in those areas. For example, if your solution was the second ad shown, ranked fourth as an organic result, and was listed as the third option on Capterra or G2, odds are that you would get a lot of traffic from those keywords.

With customers leveraging AI platforms for the long-tail of

self-education, the real estate moved and changed. You now have to:

- Show up in the AI Overviews
- Come up for the long-tail of self-education on platforms like ChatGPT and Gemini
- Still be one of the top three to four ads on Google
- Still be one of the next five to ten organic links
- Still rank on the listing sites

The problem, however, is that even with additional real estate, AI has an almost deflationary effect on organic and paid performance. It's not like more people are suddenly in the market to buy field service management software. They are just looking in more places.

The Zero-Click Searches from AI Overviews and the long-tail of self-education are reducing how much these people are interacting with companies. Instead of going to websites or talking to sales reps to educate themselves, they are using AI to bypass the entire inbound funnel and go straight to the brand with the highest recall and affinity.

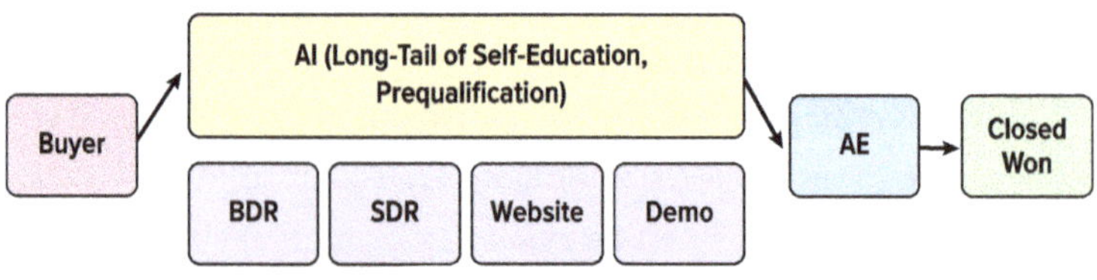

This is why paid media is much later in this process. You cannot bypass the process of building a brand and skip to investing heavily in paid media because your CAC will go through the roof as you try to compete with better brands.

"With a growing brand like ServiceFlow, however, the opposite starts to become true," I explained to Peter and Sarah. "We can be super aggressive with our paid media spend because the brand we've been building will carry our performance through."

I sat down with Sarah to analyze which campaigns she was actively running. ServiceFlow was only investing in:

- Branded Search (e.g., ServiceFlow software)
- Late Funnel Search Ads (e.g., Field Service Management Software)
- Retargeting on social platforms

With the cuts to spend, Peter had asked Sarah to make, their overall paid media budget had come down to just under $700,000 per year. All benchmarks for companies doing $25 million in revenue will tell you that $700,000 in paid media spend is far too low.

"This is not nearly enough," I said to Peter. "We need to max out our visibility on all platforms to max out the return on what we've invested in our brand."

"What's the right amount for us to be spending on paid media?" asked Peter.

"A rough ballpark figure is to be around 7–10 percent of revenue for paid media spend," I answered. "For ServiceFlow, that means we should be spending anywhere from $1.75 million to $2.5 million per year."

In my previous books, *Post-Acquisition Marketing* and *Exit-Ready Marketing*, I expanded extensively on the idea of working your way backwards through the buyer journey on every channel as the correct order of operations. Start with people who are most ready to buy, and work your way backward to those who are not yet in the market.

For paid media, this looks something like this:

Work backward on every channel

Channel	Unaware	Awareness	Knowledge	Consideration
Paid Media	• Test campaigns on nontraditional platforms (Reddit, Quora, etc.) • Test nontraditional paid channels (industry newsletters, paid PR, etc.)	• Early-funnel campaigns on Google • Cold audiences on LinkedIn and Facebook • Early-funnel content promos on paid social • Indirect categories on Capterra, G2, etc.	• Competitor campaigns on Google • Mid-funnel offers on LinkedIn and Facebook • Persona/ABM targeting on LinkedIn • Adjacent categories on Capterra, G2, Software Advice	• Branded and late-funnel campaigns on Google • Retargeting on LinkedIn, YouTube, FB, and Instagram • Capterra, G2, Software Advice direct categories

Historically, all companies would be limited to this set of campaigns because there were only a limited number of places to run campaigns. Not only that, but a bunch of campaigns like early-funnel cold audience targeting didn't work as well because companies didn't have the requisite content to make them effective.

ServiceFlow, however, had already invested extensively in content, unlike most companies. With its podcast, book, content amplification model, and social presence, ServiceFlow has a massive library of content to leverage.

Because of the deflationary nature of AI platforms and the impact of brand, the value of paid media is in increasing distribution to drive more Brand Recall and Affinity. ServiceFlow found itself in the fortunate position to capitalize on this asymmetry in the market. This meant:

1. Investing in every platform where customers could potentially encounter the ServiceFlow brand
2. Leveraging as many of our core content assets to drive consumption to increase brand affinity
3. Amplifying organic social content to increase reach and build a bigger following

This is how companies can find scale for paid media, regardless of their average deal size, sales cycle, or target market.

I worked with Sarah to build a comprehensive paid media roadmap for ServiceFlow across Google, Meta, LinkedIn, Reddit, YouTube, and X. With the help of the How To SaaS team, we first maximized all the standard late-funnel campaigns on all platforms. Then we started leveraging the podcast, product tools, the book, and all other assets for earlier stages of the funnel.

What this looked like in practice:

- We maxed out all late funnel, mid funnel, and early funnel campaigns on paid search
- We maxed out retargeting on Google, YouTube, LinkedIn, Meta, and X
- We maxed out listings advertising on Capterra, G2, and all other platforms
- We maxed out mid-funnel and early-funnel campaigns on

LinkedIn, Meta, Reddit, X, and YouTube, often promoting social content that was performing quite well to grow the audience
- We maxed out mid-funnel and early-funnel campaigns to core content properties—specifically the *Field Service Champions* podcast and *The Field Service Growth Playbook*—to build out the audience further
- We maxed out early funnel campaigns to core pain points resolved through short-form pieces of content on LinkedIn, Meta, Reddit, X, and YouTube

We also expanded into different forms of paid distribution:

- We paid influencers and content creators to promote core ServiceFlow assets and thought leadership content
- We paid a PR agency to get us placements on business podcasts for Peter to talk about *The Field Service Growth Playbook* and to promote how to build a field service business
- We paid for sponsored promos on podcasts and YouTube channels that focused on technical knowledge for plumbers, electricians, landscapers, and roofers
- We sponsored conferences for field service companies, including having Peter speak at those conferences

Paid Media Roadmap	Channel	Action
Maxing Out the Core	Paid search	Maxed-out late-funnel, mid-funnel, and early-funnel campaigns
	Paid social—LinkedIn, Meta, Reddit, X, and YouTube	Maxed-out: • Retargeting • Mid-funnel and early-funnel campaigns, often promoting high-promoting social content that grew the audience • Early-funnel campaigns to short-form content on core pain points
	Review sites	Maxed-out listings advertising on Capterra, G2, and all other platforms
	Core content properties	Maxed-out mid-funnel and early-funnel campaigns to core content properties to build out the audience further
Expanding Paid Distribution	Influencers and content creators	Promoted core ServiceFlow assets and thought leadership content
	PR	Paid an agency to get us placements on business podcasts for Peter to talk about the Field Service Growth Playbook and to promote how to build a field service business
	Podcasts and YouTube channels	Paid for sponsored promos that focused on technical knowledge for plumbers, electricians, landscapers, and roofers
	Events	Sponsored conferences for field service companies, including speaking opportunities

This investment was extensive. ServiceFlow's investment in paid media spend jumped to $2 million with all of these channels and campaigns.

It became a virtuous cycle. Sarah and her team executed on the playbook to scale the podcast and organic reach, then amplified everything with paid media. The result was that the podcast started growing faster, ServiceFlow's and Peter's following grew, thousands of prospects were interacting with the free tools, Peter started to get even more speaking opportunities and Branded Search Volume and Direct Traffic skyrocketed.

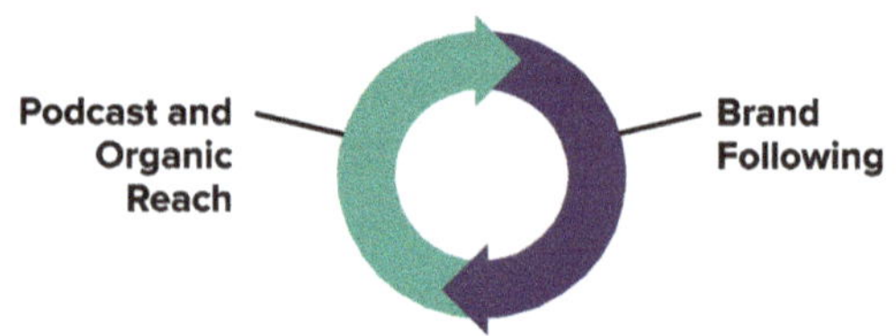

Visibility on AI platforms also increased. Paid media had amplified an engine that was already getting a ton of credibility from AI platforms.

TYPE OF QUERY	VISIBILITY START (%)	VISIBILITY NOW (%)
Navigational	72%	89%
Informational	12%	52%
Transactional	36%	73%
Generative	5%	42%

"There's one more important step that we need to do here," I said to both of them. "We need to future-proof this performance like an asset so that we don't lose it again."

"How do we do that?" asked Peter.

"By ensuring we are tracking the right metrics and making adjustments as we go along."

MEASURING AND FUTURE-PROOFING PERFORMANCE

The business impact of the increase in spend was clearly visible as well. In *Post-Acquisition Marketing* and *Exit-Ready Marketing*, I walked through an extensive process for measuring and scaling media. Instead of expanding on it here again, I will simplify things here to say that I had Sarah track the following metrics for all campaigns and channels for paid media spend:

- Spend
- Leads
- MQLs
- Cost/MQL
- SALs
- Opportunities
- Cost/Opportunity
- Closed Won deals
- CAC

On the increased spend, ServiceFlow saw an overall increase in pipeline and revenue from paid media of over 237 percent, and CAC Payback was under 16 months. This business impact was not just the result of increasing the paid media spend. It was the downstream impact of investing heavily in the brand and Iconic Positioning for ServiceFlow.

"I've never been this thrilled to be wrong," said Peter.

Sarah was also happy. She had been struggling to convince Peter to ramp up spending in paid media for a while, and now there were results to help her scale that even more.

"The brand and position we've established is the moat here," I said to Peter and Sarah. "We must constantly stay on top of how we are doing when it comes to those numbers."

The metrics listed previously do not account for this additional layer of complexity. I get asked this question all the time. How do you figure out what's working for paid media when people are often choosing solutions based on brands?

For example, if someone searches for CRM software and buys Salesforce, it doesn't seem right that paid search gets all the credit, does it? The buyer could have heard Marc Benioff speak, attended Dreamforce, watched a Salesforce webinar, already been a customer of Slack, or partnered with a Revenue Operations agency in the Salesforce ecosystem.

In a world with AI, this attribution problem is further amplified by the fact that people are self-educating in the long-tail and engaging with all kinds of social media content. The goal here, then, is not to have the best attribution model. Instead, we must track additional metrics to see how we are trending for KPIs on our overall brand.

I had Sarah build out a dashboard to track how we were performing for the following:

- Branded Search Volume
- Branded Mentions on Social
- Visibility Percentage for AI queries we want to rank for
- NPS ratings
- CSAT ratings
- Podcast downloads

- Podcast subscribers
- YouTube subscribers
- Minutes watched on YouTube
- Social Media interactions
- Book sales
- Engagement with top-of-funnel product tools
- Podcast guest appearances per month
- Speaking opportunities per month
- PR coverages and mentions per month

Brand Dashboard	Month 1	Month 2	M/M	Month 3	M/M	Q1 Total
Branded search volume						
Branded mentions on social						
Visibility % for AI queries we want to rank for						
NPS ratings						
CSAT ratings						
Podcast downloads						
Podcast subscribers						
YouTube subscribers						
Minutes watched on YouTube						
Social media interactions						
Book sales						
Engagement with top-of-funnel product tools						
Podcast guest appearances per month						
Speaking opportunities per month						
PR coverages and mentions per month						

Suddenly, there was so much more to track for the business.

"What do you notice about this list of metrics?" I asked Sarah.

"None of them are directly connected to sales funnel metrics," she answered.

"Doesn't this put us at a risk of getting consumed by vanity metrics?" asked Peter.

"It can, yes," I confirmed. "But in a world with AI, we must look at both these metrics and our funnel metrics to triangulate what is working."

In my previous books, I had drawn very specific boundaries around what should be measured and counted in terms of overall marketing impact, and I emphasized the importance of tying everything to revenue. All those metrics are still critical and take priority.

However, in a world with AI, the metrics listed above are leading indicators of how your sales pipeline will perform in the future. Visibility percentage for AI queries is the most obvious example. If your visibility metrics decline, your sales funnel performance will likely follow suit. The same is true for all the other metrics on that list.

Again, AI platforms are looking for signals on how to answer one critical question: What is the best possible answer to this query, and *who* has the best possible answer to this question?

If AI queries continue to grow over the next 5 years, there will come a time when these leading indicators will be the primary signals that help us understand why AI platforms cite some sources over others. These leading indicators will also tell us how our brand is trending and help us understand why our paid media efficiency is changing.

Also, consider this: what if more competitors ran the same play-book we ran with ServiceFlow? Similar to SEO, showing up in AI queries once again becomes a battleground for real estate.

Alternatively, what happens in a world where you can run ads on ChatGPT or Gemini queries? No one knows exactly what this will look like. But you'll see sponsored answers alongside organic ones. Maybe it will be a paid citation that appears to be an organic result.

In both cases, building the brand and tracking performance beyond direct funnel metrics becomes critical to protecting the moat that the investment in brand and Iconic Positioning has built. In a world like that, there will be even more noise to cut through. Organic results will need to be even stronger and show-case even more expertise or referenceability.

With the new dashboards we set up with Sarah, ServiceFlow was now set up for success to track and improve its performance over time.

"We have one last step remaining," I said to Peter.

"What's that?" he asked.

"We need to update ServiceFlow's sales process."

YOUR TURN

6. Paid Distribution

Choose one to two paid media channels to invest in to amplify the reach, visibility, and brand recall and affinity of your content and solution.

Follow these prompts to build an initial list:

- What content, if amplified, will help you build your brand in the marketplace?
- Which channels are best for finding your ICP so they can interact with your content?
- What is the right order of channels and campaigns to work through?

Get the full workbook at: www.howtosaas.com/blueprint.

CHAPTER 7

BUILDING A NEW SALES PLAYBOOK

1. Prequalification	2. Iconic Positioning	3. Citation-Worthy Content	4. Authenticity and Originality
Create a list of fifteen to twenty-five long-tail self-education queries to prequalify your ICP.	Create a list of five to ten adjacent problem areas your ICP is facing beyond the scope of your solution.	Identify one Anchor Content Property you will heavily invest into as a way to signal your expertise.	Build one proprietary process, framework, or approach to help your ICP navigate their core pain points.

5. Product Levers	6. Paid Distribution	7. Sales Plays
Identify three to five product tools that can help your ICP solve their problems without necessarily buying your full solution.	Choose one to two paid media channels to invest into to amplify the reach, visibility, brand recall, and affinity of your content and solution.	Prioritize three to five sales plays built around intent signals and cocreating content with your ICP to scale outreach, especially higher-value accounts.

Download at howtosaas.com/blueprint

"How does the sales team prioritize deals?" I asked Peter.

"We focus on inbound sales for the most part," he answered. "The team prioritizes the biggest opportunities with the highest likelihood of closing and works their way through the list."

"What about outbound?" I asked.

"We do some of this," said Peter. "Mostly, we are cold calling lists of field service companies."

"How has that been performing?" I asked.

"Performance has been declining," he said. "We used to get much higher connect and response rates. But these last 12 months have been much slower for outbound."

"That's one of the reasons why we've focused even more on inbound," said Matt, chiming in. Matt was ServiceFlow's VP of Sales. "We let go of a couple of our lower-performing outbound reps last month."

Peter and Matt had described how a lot of companies do outbound—finding pipeline and revenue through volume. Over time, in almost all companies, performance declines, reps have lesser success, and VPs of sales are fired.

Why? Because everyone is looking for someone to blame. The reality is that there is no one to blame. The sales process just doesn't work.

The reason a lot of outbound programs fail is that there are a few critical elements missing. The outbound teams often dial for prospects who:

- Are not actually in the ICP of what the company is selling
- Are not big enough to make the economics of outbound work
- Do not actually need the solution
- Do not have the budget for the solution
- Do not have the decision-making authority for the solution
- Do not need the solution at the present moment

Between these factors, a large majority of outbound programs either fail or are significantly more inefficient than they should be.

In a world with AI, this problem gets amplified:

- In the long-tail of self-education, customers do not engage with companies till much later in the buying process
- As experts in each market are revealed, pipeline shifts to companies with stronger Brand Recall and Affinity
- Outbound and inbound efficiency declines for companies that do not have stronger brands, with rising competition and higher CAC payback periods

Commoditization of content through AI only makes things worse. Companies are deploying "agents" to increase the volume of outreach through email, phone calls, and LinkedIn. Companies have resorted to leveraging AI as a way to fire their sales reps while still doing outbound through these agents.

Agents, automation, and AI all have a place in the sales process of companies. This is not to say that they are not valid. Sadly, this is not the way to make it work better.

"With all the work we've been doing on the marketing side to grow the ServiceFlow brand, we need to be much more intentional with our sales efforts," I said to Peter and Matt.

"What's the right way to go about it?" asked Matt.

"We need to focus on the highest value deals we can actually win."

FOCUSING SALES EFFORTS ON THE RIGHT ACCOUNTS

We went back to some of the metrics Peter had shared earlier. As customers were self-serving their way through AI platforms, ServiceFlow had seen the following:

- Close rates had jumped from 30 percent to 40 percent
- Average deal sizes had increased by 15 percent
- Sales cycles had decreased by 50 percent
- First-year retention had improved from 92 percent to 97 percent

The customers that were coming inbound were already being prequalified and converting at higher rates. Across its top verticals, here is how the numbers looked.

Vertical	Win Rates	ACV	NRR
Roofing/Construction	55%	$15,000	110%
Plumbing/Electrical/HVAC	45%	$12,000	107%
Landscaping	40%	$18,000	105%

"Let's take this a step further," I said to Peter, Matt, and Sarah. "Let's map out how big the universe of target accounts is."

"That number is in the tens of thousands," said Peter. "Each state and region has thousands of these companies."

"I'm more interested in the larger ones," I explained. "How many target accounts would be worth more than $75,000 per year to ServiceFlow?"

"That universe is definitely a lot smaller," said Peter.

In *Exit-Ready Marketing*, I explained that the first area of maturity companies need to build out is truly understanding their ICP and mapping their TAM. In ServiceFlow's case, they had a very good idea of their ideal buyers. What they hadn't done was focus their sales efforts on the larger deals where they could get the best ROI.

I worked with Matt and Sarah to illustrate how big the potential revenue opportunity was from these larger accounts that were worth more than $75,000 per year. Here is what we found:

Vertical	Customers	Total Market	Penetration
Roofing/Construction	45	732	6.1%
Plumbing/Electrical/HVAC	71	1,293	5.5%
Landscaping	24	537	4.4%

This analysis highlighted that ServiceFlow had a market penetration of less than 7 percent for large accounts across its top verticals. What's more is that most of these firms were not on a competitor solution. About 95 percent of the market was a true greenfield opportunity, with a revenue opportunity of over $250 million for just these accounts.

When we looked at how many of these deals ServiceFlow was closing per year, it was less than ten. In most years, ServiceFlow only closed seven to eight enterprise accounts. Everything else was inbound.

"These are the accounts we really need to focus on with our outbound efforts," I explained to Peter and Matt. "But we also need to build a sales process that leverages AI as a strength."

Traditionally, a lot of companies do TAM analysis like this and then revert to cold calling as their go-to approach for sales. This leads to companies having the same issues ServiceFlow was having before—ineffective outreach to accounts that don't engage or close.

"We need to be much more intentional about which accounts we focus on with our sales efforts," I continued.

"How do we do that?" asked Matt.

"We need to connect our outreach efforts with the work we've been doing with our content based on intent data and signals."

USING CONTENT FOR INTENT DATA AND SIGNALS

One reason outbound doesn't work is that Marketing and Sales do not work together to target the same accounts.

Around 2019, this started to change. Companies started to focus on Account-Based Marketing (ABM) as one of their main Go-To-Market strategies. The idea was to create customized content for a top list of named accounts and have sales and marketing target those accounts across all kinds of channels. This led to millions of dollars in investment in people, tech stack, and processes to give ABM a proper shot.

When I meet a lot of these companies, they often haven't figured out the unit economics around ABM. It works a bit better than general outbound, but often inefficiently considering the giant costs associated with running ABM programs.

The reason why companies have trouble figuring this out is that ABM programs often focus on larger target ICP accounts, with deal sizes that are often north of $100,000 in annual value. With deal sizes so large, a lot of criteria need to be met before a deal will actually close:

- The account must be in the market for the solution
- They must have the budget and willingness to pay
- They must have the urgency
- They must have internal buy-in from other stakeholders

These characteristics are often difficult to manufacture by simply sending out custom content to larger accounts. For example, you cannot create urgency for a large landscaping company to buy ServiceFlow to improve their project management, dispatching, scheduling, and invoicing. They have to be in a buying window to take on such an infrastructure project.

To solve this problem, a lot of platforms have emerged to fill the gap of targeting the right accounts at the right time. Clay is probably the best example of this as it has grown at a record pace to satisfy this need inside sales organizations. Tools like this are invaluable to improve sales efficiency and increase conversions by tracking things like:

- Website visits by target accounts
- Job changes by ICP
- News related to companies (e.g., acquisitions)

You can then run workflows and orchestrations against these kinds of timely triggers, which is significantly better than random cold outbound.

However, these kinds of intent data and enrichment platforms do not complete the full cycle of what really closes deals. Brand, content, social, and engagement are such a critical part of entering these sales conversations at the right time. For example, you could be selling a CRM platform and pull a list of target accounts, enrich them with an intent platform, and build better orchestration and automation, but prospects may still choose Salesforce. Why? Because the brand is that powerful.

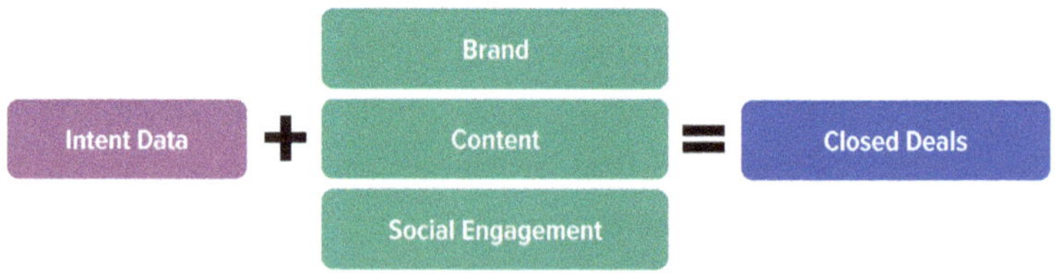

In a world with AI, this gets pushed into overdrive: AI platforms are citing experts and helping customers self-educate for the long-tail, buyers are consuming content (video, podcasts, reels, etc.) on social media. A lot of the buyer journey becomes even more invisible to intent data platforms.

"This is where the content we are producing is so critical," I explained to Peter, Matt, and Sarah.

"How can our content help us with outreach?" asked Matt.

"Our content is creating signals no one else in the market has access to," I answered.

By aggressively investing in content, ServiceFlow had created a barrage of new signals for its brand:

- Followers on podcasts, YouTube, and social channels
- Peter's connections on LinkedIn, Twitter, and Instagram
- Podcast subscribers
- Book purchasers
- Reactions, engagements, and comments on social content or social ads
- Direct messages and chats on all social platforms
- Audiences of events, webinars, and podcasts where Peter had spoken

As Peter, Sarah, and the team produced more content, even more signals emerged. Not all were necessarily buying signals. But the people interacting with the content were avid followers of Peter and ServiceFlow. They had an affinity for the brand.

I had Sarah and Matt build processes to sift through these people, workflows, and automations that piggybacked on all the content we were producing. When we cross-referenced these content signals against the target accounts we had prioritized, there was a clear overlap. About 5–7 percent of our target accounts were interacting with the content monthly. Each month, new overlaps would become visible.

When Matt and Sarah layered this data on top of standard intent signals to prioritize accounts, they had a clear shortlist of accounts to prioritize on a monthly basis. Outbound at ServiceFlow became a mix of email, phone, and social outreach. Social outreach in particular outperformed email and phone in terms of conversion rates. Overall pipeline from outbound also increased to the point where the economics started to make sense again.

Most importantly, ServiceFlow had turned its content engine into a sales playbook beyond its standard operations.

"This has changed how I look at this whole initiative," said Peter. "Till now, I thought this was just a marketing project. By working on the sales process, we've turned this into an end-to-end revenue initiative."

Peter was exactly right. This is the same change all organizations need to make in a world with AI. Sales cannot depend solely on processes separate from Marketing. Instead, it needs to be connected to the engine driving the brand and visibility.

"There's one critical step that will increase the ROI on this work," I said.

"What's that?" asked Peter.

"We need to leverage our core assets to co-create content with our ICP."

CO-CREATING CONTENT WITH THE ICP

"So far, our sales work has been downstream from our content," I explained.

"What do you mean by that?" asked Peter.

"We first create the content, then we leverage intent signals to deploy sales plays," I answered. "We need to start leveraging sales activities to drive content."

One of the biggest missed opportunities inside most companies is that they don't work with their potential customers to create content and core assets together. In ServiceFlow's case, Peter was often interviewing existing customers to get their perspective on how to grow a field service company. What he wasn't doing was interviewing target accounts to build relationships with potential customers.

"This is where the content playbook we've been running really starts to generate immediate returns," I continued.

I asked Matt and Sarah to combine their target account lists with the intent signals we had identified through our content. We then split out the interactions into three tiers:

- Tier 1: ICP accounts, high intent, high value—these accounts entered directly into sales conversations.

- Tier 2: ICP accounts, low to medium intent, high value—these accounts became prime candidates to engage in a content co-creation cycle
- Tier 3: Non-ICP accounts—these accounts were pushed much lower down the priority list

Target Account Tier	Intent Signals	Action
Tier 1: ICP Accounts	High intent, high value	These accounts entered directly into sales conversations
Tier 2: ICP Accounts	Low to medium intent, high value	These accounts became prime candidates to engage into a content cocreation cycle
Tier 3: Non-ICP Accounts	Low value	These accounts were pushed much lower down the priority list

For Tier 1 accounts, it made no sense to disrupt the sales cycle by having them come on the podcast. For Tier 2 accounts, however, there wasn't an immediate sales opportunity, but there was such a great fit with ServiceFlow that investing in the account had tremendous long-term benefits.

Matt and Sarah started leveraging this playbook to invite prospects onto the *Field Service Champions* podcast. The sales process was simple:

1. Invite ICP accounts on the podcast
2. Build relationships through the co-creation of content for the podcast
3. Actively co-promote the content together with the guest
4. Promote the content through all of ServiceFlow's social accounts to give the guest value
5. Build a sales follow-up process behind publishing the episode and content

With this simple playbook, ServiceFlow tripled the number of enterprise deals it started to close every year. Instead of closing eight per year, ServiceFlow started closing almost thirty from the guests on the podcast alone. This was on top of the intent-based ABM work it was doing with Tier 1 accounts.

By having Sales leverage their content as a way to nurture relationships, ServiceFlow uncovered something that most companies overlook. A way to find scale with content is to produce content that plays double duty or triple duty. For example, when ServiceFlow interviewed a large potential buyer on the *Field Service Champions* podcast, it was creating product marketing content, thought leadership content, sales enablement content, and content that would increase its credibility with AI platforms.

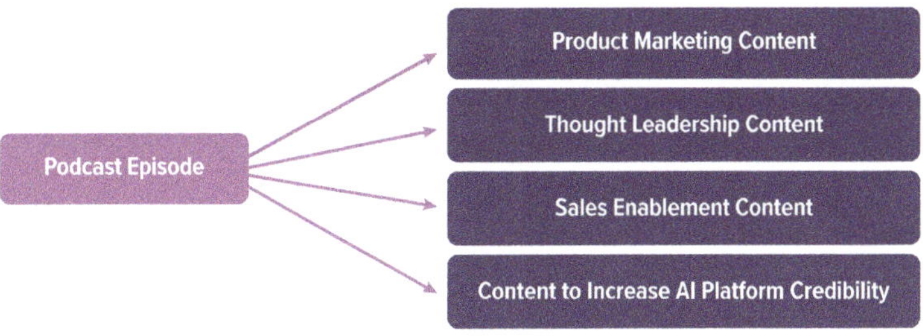

The initiatives feed each other. The podcast creates Iconic Positioning for ServiceFlow, which increases AI visibility, which builds the brand, which increases interactions, which increases intent signals, which increases the number of ICP customers that can be invited on the podcast, which creates more pipeline.

The ROI from this work gave Sarah, Matt, and Peter significantly more confidence to keep investing in content that was helpful.

Suddenly, ServiceFlow had a business case to increase its investment in its Iconic Positioning even further.

Instead of publishing one episode per week, ServiceFlow started publishing five episodes per week, each with a potential buyer. As ServiceFlow ramped up its publishing schedule across all platforms in the form of full podcasts and the resulting micro content, its visibility metrics reached new highs.

TYPE OF QUERY	VISIBILITY START (%)	VISIBILITY NOW (%)
Navigational	72%	89%
Informational	12%	67%
Transactional	36%	78%
Generative	5%	57%

"The returns from this work have surpassed all of my expectations," said Peter.

"The key is to keep going," I responded. "The market is going to get increasingly competitive the more AI evolves."

Peter nodded in agreement, "We have to stay the course to maintain this position."

ServiceFlow had become a leader in the market. There was a clear trajectory to becoming a $100 million company. And there was no chance Peter was giving that up.

7. Sales Plays

Prioritize three to five sales plays built around intent signals and co-creating content with your ICP to scale outreach, especially higher-value accounts.

Follow these prompts to build an initial list:

- Which intent signals should you use to track and trigger outreach?
- How can you identify and target higher-value accounts with your content?
- How can you co-create content with your ICP?

Get the full workbook at: www.howtosaas.com/blueprint.

CONCLUSION

	Visibility Before	Visibility After Iconic Positioning	Visibility After Social Distribution	Visibility After Original Content	Visibility After Generative Query List	Visibility After Leveraging Product	Visibility After Paid Media	Visibility After Updating Sales Process
Navigational	72%	78%	83%	89%	89%	89%	89%	89%
Informational	12%	17%	29%	45%	45%	45%	52%	67%
Transactional	36%	39%	55%	68%	68%	68%	73%	78%
Generative	5%	9%	12%	17%	12%	35%	42%	57%

Peter kept the business focused for the next 12 months. Sarah and Matt continued executing on the playbook we had built together, and the business grew as a result:

- ServiceFlow's podcast grew to 5,000 downloads per episode
- Visibility metrics on AI platforms climbed past 60 percent
- YoY Growth increased from 15 percent to 40 percent
- NRR improved from 105 percent to 115 percent
- New ARR grew by 2.5 times to $6.25 million per year

- Sales Pipeline almost doubled to $15.6 million
- Ending ARR grew to $35 million

Beyond all this, the ServiceFlow brand and Peter's following grew extensively with all the work that had been done.

"It's funny," said Peter. "This whole time we talked about this like a project focused on AI platforms, but this was really a business transformation project."

"You're 100 percent right," I agreed. "The AI platforms have just given us the impetus we needed to start doing the highest value work for ServiceFlow."

Peter's insight is something I think all founders can learn from. You are not trying to just rank for more terms on AI platforms. This isn't about GEO. This is about a whole new way to think about your customers and business.

The emergence of AI and future developments should change how you think about marketing, product, sales, customers, positioning, and brand. And rightfully so. The companies that grow the fastest in this market will be the ones that take on the challenge of helping their customers in a world with AI.

The frameworks in this book, if followed vigorously, will compound over time for any business in any market. At How To SaaS, we've helped thousands of clients navigate such changes and transformations and see phenomenal results over condensed periods of time.

If you are a CEO, investor, or executive who wants to take your company's marketing function through the kind of transformation we took Peter and ServiceFlow through, schedule a consult at www.howtosaas.com to see how we can help your business scale faster.

RESOURCES

You can download the full AI Marketing Blueprint workbook at www.howtosaas.com/blueprint

Included in the workbook:

- One-page overview template to summarize your holistic plan
- Separate worksheets for each box of the blueprint that correspond with the chapters in this book
- Prompts and fillable sections to help you complete the roadmap for your business

1. Prequalification	**2. Iconic Positioning**	**3. Citation-Worthy Content**	**4. Authenticity and Originality**
Create a list of fifteen to twenty-five long-tail self-education queries to prequalify your ICP.	*Create a list of five to ten adjacent problem areas your ICP is facing beyond the scope of your solution.*	*Identify one Anchor Content Property you will heavily invest into as a way to signal your expertise.*	*Build one proprietary process, framework, or approach to help your ICP navigate their core pain points.*

5. Product Levers	**6. Paid Distribution**	**7. Sales Plays**
Identify three to five product tools that can help your ICP solve their problems without necessarily buying your full solution.	*Choose one to two paid media channels to invest into to amplify the reach, visibility, brand recall, and affinity of your content and solution.*	*Prioritize three to five sales plays built around intent signals and cocreating content with your ICP to scale outreach, especially higher-value accounts.*

Download at howtosaas.com/blueprint

ACKNOWLEDGMENTS

I'd like to thank the following people, who were essential in my journey to building the frameworks, experiences, and expertise shared in this book:

- Zane Tarence, Partner and Managing Director at Founders Advisors
- Michael Libert, Managing Director at TA Associates
- Donald Cowper, COO at How To SaaS
- Kate Hawkes, VP of Marketing at How To SaaS
- Our entire team at How To SaaS, with whom the concepts in this book were built
- Our clients at How To SaaS, whom we get the pleasure of serving every day
- My daughter, Lyla, for inspiring me to chase my dreams